A JOHN CATT
PUBLICATION

BORN TO FAIL?

SOCIAL MOBILITY:
A WORKING CLASS VIEW

SONIA BLANDFORD

FOREWORD BY
RT. HON. DAVID LAWS

First Published 2017

by John Catt Educational Ltd,
15 Riduna Park, Station Road,
Melton, Woodbridge IP12 1QT

Tel: +44 (0) 1394 389850
Email: enquiries@johncatt.com
Website: www.johncatt.com

ISBN: 978 1 1911382409

Set and designed by John Catt Educational Limited

Praise for *Born to Fail?*

'Sonia Blandford's book hit me like a ducking in freezing water. My starting point was the opposite to hers – privileged and certain I could change the world. She says of the working class, 'it isn't about rescuing them. It's about valuing them and allowing them to develop in their own way'. Written with great clarity and personal insight, this is a book which if taken seriously, especially by educationists and policy makers, really could change the world and I personally wish I had had the benefits of its wisdom fifty years ago. It is a perfect read for anyone wanting to see a more equitable society in modern Britain.'

Sir Stephen O'Brien CBE (Founding Chair Teach First; Founding CEO Business in the Community and London First)

'Blandford may be the first Professor to have failed her English qualification five times – but this heart-ripping, brain-provoking book uses words perfectly to explain why class is not the same as disadvantage, why social mobility isn't something well-educated teachers can hand to chosen children but is something every child must be helped to choose for themselves, and why something as simple as playing the cornet in a school musical can be life-changing. Practical, hard-hitting, and packed with evidence, this is a manifesto for looking again at how we really make schools work for everyone.'

Laura McInerney, Editor of *Schools Week*

'This book offers a genuinely new and unique approach to the debate on social mobility by using the author's own experience of growing up and succeeding from a working class background. Sonia shows how we need to understand the impact of working class experience and values on learners if we are to successfully shape educational policy and interventions which really have a chance of success. Building on her own extensive experience of implementing life changing programmes in education she explores what needs to change in our system to turn around the fact that social mobility is going backwards. This is a must read analysis if you are interested in making a difference in this area.'

Brian Lamb, OBE (Special Educational Needs and Disability policy expert and Government adviser)

'Too often, the term 'social mobility' is about uprooting. But by insisting that it is about 'life improvement and life chances' rather than 'class migration', Professor Blandford's book provides a much needed alternative conception. *Born to Fail?* is deeply rooted in Blandford's personal and professional experience and by sharing her own journey she takes the reader on a journey themselves. This makes Blanfdord's argument refreshing, readable, passionate and personal. This practical and impassioned analysis will help any reader increase the sophistication of their understanding whilst galvanising their commitment to change.'

Loic Menzies, CEO, LKMco

'*Born to Fail?* resonates, from its opening lines, with authenticity, honesty and insight. These for me remain its key themes, and heightened relevance in shaping the connected, coordinated and co-constructed strategies that must now be developed within and alongside the communities whose potential will only be further released through a genuine sense of ownership of them. 'By and with', not 'for and to' are key messages that need to heeded from this crucial work if social injustice is to be effectively – and genuinely – tackled. Engagement, an emphasis on mutuality, rooted in a unique combination of personal experience and professional practice, is indeed the counterpoint to Sonia's compelling arguments for a redefinition of the issue, our thinking about it and the actions which are now essential to address what cannot continue to be the unanswered question of this, as well as so many previous generations.'

Derek Peaple (Headteacher, Park House School, West Berkshire; 2016 *TES* Headteacher of the year finalist)

'A book such as this should not be necessary in 2017, given that it picks up themes identified over half a century ago, but Professor Blandford is quite right in showing that we as a society still have some way to go. Sonia writes from a position of authority, thanks not only to her background and personal experience of many of the issues she talks about, but also through the tremendous work she has done with people who continue to be overlooked or underserved in society.

This book is important in showing us as teachers that the way forward is bigger than what we as a profession alone can achieve, but that we all must be part of solution if anything is to change. I hope that a work of this kind is not needed in another 50 years, thanks to the foundation for action and understanding that this book can help to provide.'

Paul Dwyer (Deputy Headteacher, North London Collegiate School; Chair, Chartered College of Teaching)

'A thought provoking powerful personal account of the author's childhood and professional career, it illustrats the importance of the difference we can make by working in co-production with families and wider partners which is at the heart of the Children and Families Act 2014. This book is highly relevant as we continue to face the challenges of addressing disadvantaged children and young people. A must read for all families and professionals!'

Sherann Hillman MBE Head of Family Services Seashell Trust, National Network of Parent Carer Forum (NNPCF) National Rep and Chair of Stockport's parent carer forum. Previously Co-Chair and NW rep of NNPCF

'This is a wonderful and inspiring book. Sonia Blandford has written a moving and compelling manifesto for social justice and mobility. There are practical solutions to achieve social mobility for working class children and those children and families struggling with entrenched disadvantage. Breaking intergenerational disadvantage is a concern for educationalists, politicians and parents. This book reveals how much social disadvantage costs the United Kingdom financially and socially and details the human and societal cost of low aspiration, poverty and barriers to the development of the whole child. As she notes, if children are our investment in the future, everyone should have a stake in their welfare.'

Catherine Roche, CEO, Place2Be

'There has been little progress in the last fifty years for the most disadvantaged members of our society in the UK. *Born to Fail?* is a deeply personal, often moving and highly relevant call to arms from Blandford to challenge this 'social injustice of our times'. She reflects honestly on her working class 1970's childhood in west London, weaving her story with evidence from research, to illuminate how little has changed for children from similar backgrounds to her own. Blandford reminds us that social mobility is not about class migration, but the improvement of life choices and chances for all. Mutuality may have been overlooked, but it is not too late for us to engage with working class values and develop partnerships early on between parents, carers and teachers so that everyone can succeed.'

Professor Tanya Ovenden-Hope, Professor of Education, Plymouth Marjon University

'*Born to Fail?* is a powerful manifesto for change, which encourages us to think differently about social mobility in this country. As well as a personal and moving account of Professor Sonia Blandford's own journey, this book is full of real-life stories from schools and charities across the UK and draws on insights and data from other important research studies. *Born to Fail?* shows how a more holistic, inclusive and kind approach to education can bring about the change we need.'

Russell Speirs, Founder and CEO, RSAcademics

'My sister Sonia's book details the importance of valuing working class consciousness, demonstrating that you CAN achieve from a zero start in life. Gaining confidence from performing in brass and military bands at prestigious events helped define my abilities. Joining the many working class mature students at The Open University provided me and our brother Ian the opportunity to gain degrees, proving that we and our peers were not Born to Fail.'

Susan Blandford BA Hons. DIP Mus, Peripatetic music teacher, textiles expert

Contents

This book is dedicated to my children.
My hope is that their generation will see and experience a positive
move towards social justice for all in the years ahead.

Foreword

Born to Fail? takes a fresh look at one of the greatest challenges facing our society – how can we break the strong and enduring link between life chances and family background and circumstances?

The book benefits not just from Professor Blandford's detailed understanding of recent educational and social research, but from her own perspectives and personal experience.

Why is the progress on social mobility so frustratingly slow? Why are some of the most disadvantaged pupils falling even further behind? And are middle class assumptions about working class expectations realistic and grounded in real world aspirations?

The merit of this book is that it does not seek to dismiss the value of specific educational interventions or assume that poverty will inevitably cap aspirations and attainment. Poverty should not be allowed to be an excuse for poor quality education or low expectations. The best schools really can make a profound difference to life chances.

But Professor Blandford also understands that education cannot be considered in isolation if we want to make a truly meaningful impact on social mobility. Parental support, the learning environment outside the school or college, and each individual's engagement and motivation are all important too.

This wider understanding helps explain the challenging circumstances in which educationalists are seeking to close the attainment and opportunity gap, as inequality in wealth, income, home and work circumstances remains stubbornly persistent or even increases in some societies.

The causes of our disadvantaged gap are many. This book gives a real sense both of the scale and nature of the challenge, as well as the range of policy changes which are needed if our country is no longer to be a place in which so many are 'Born to Fail'.

Rt. Hon. David Laws,
Executive Chairman of the Education Policy Institute; Schools
Minister 2012-2015

Preface

In July 2017, sat in my home office reflecting on the end of another full and mainly productive academic year, there was a realisation that as a working class Professor I might have something to contribute to the social mobility debate. A view that would be immersed in my experience, contributing to the class consciousness that has been subject to media activity and political debate over the last year.

Throughout my career my advice to my colleagues has been not to move into areas of practice where they have neither training or experience. Following my own advice, I would not claim to have expertise or knowledge much beyond education; a little about music perhaps. And, maybe, something about looked after children, but that would be it.

That said, born in the late 1950s, I am the product of a 1960s/70s working class family, subject to the many struggles that are now defined as disadvantaged rather than class. Based on this experience, and more, I have a view on social mobility, one which I am privileged to be able to share with you in this book.

The limitations of the book will be readily perceived, manifestly so by expert sociologists, political commentators, educators and others. Bringing together key issues that I have witnessed and researched, there is an underpinning evidence-base to points made. Each of which would happily be subject to criticism and debate. I invite you, the reader, to do so.

My aim in sharing my story and thoughts on social mobility is to question the injustice of the current prevailing view of the issue, that the working class have somehow failed and they should become more like the middle class. That is, pass the required exams to go to university, get a degree or two, buy their own house and live a healthy life, contributing to society and the economy. Not too dissimilar to my own story in some ways, but lacking the notion of family, and the tribal effect of the working class. In short, I am, and always will be, working class in my actions and deeds. My moral compass was set at birth.

My ambition for the book is that it is not read as a political statement but as an introduction to an alternative way of thinking about social mobility – a way of thinking that crucially listens to, engages and involves the working class in determining what their future should be. An alternative way that values partnership, mutuality and collaboration and which, by doing what is right, creates opportunities for all.

Chapter 1
The starting point

In the early 1950s and 60s children from the estates where I was growing up participated in a study (later published in 1973), of disadvantaged children and the enormous inequalities we suffered (health, family circumstances, educational development), compared to what the authors then called 'ordinary' children.

I would not be represented in this study as I might be now – a Professor of Education who works with the same kind of charity that led the research. Rather, my role was as a child born into a working class family in 1958 and growing up in west London in the direst of circumstances. The data for the study was gathered at three points: at birth, in primary years, and latterly in 1969 when the cohort was 11. This study was designed to paint an 'accurate' and 'reliable' picture of the conditions British children were growing up in at that time.

The children on the estates where I lived were involved because of the study's focus on comparing working class families with 'ordinary families' born in 1958.

My mother had a transient and troubled childhood, born and raised in army camps, Peabody developments in London and, finally, a member of one of the many families rehoused, post war, onto the South Oxhey estate. My grandfather, the seventh child of a shop worker, was kicked out of the forces for bigamy, and his family kicked out of their living quarters as a result. My mum had a chequered education, never properly learned to read and from her early twenties suffered from chronic depression – a condition probably triggered by the abuse she suffered and the tragic events that followed her throughout her life, including the loss of her older brother to suicide. My father's family were Welsh miners. He'd lost his own mother to suicide and for many years lived in a tent with his dad in Osterley Park in London, before they moved to South Oxhey to live with his sister when his dad was dying. He was, I can see now, angry with the world as a result of that early experience.

When he and mum met and married they moved to west London, where mum had a job working on the production line at EMI. Soon after she was pregnant with twins, my sister Susan and me, and dad picked up a permanent job as a shift worker on the production line at Technicolor. We were born into a two-room home above a sweet shop before being rehoused by the council onto the Allied Housing Estate in west London, living in a community that was part of the aforementioned study of me and my peers. The report that came out of it – *Born to Fail?*[1] – inspired the title of this book and makes interesting reading today. It asserts that:

> If it is accepted that many parents are expected to cope with impossible burdens, and that their material circumstances provide a major contribution to those burdens, then there is much to be said for tackling more earnestly the poor housing and low income that our study has revealed. Arguably it could eliminate a large part of many families' difficulties. And on humanitarian grounds alone large numbers of children need a better chance to grow, develop, learn and live than they currently receive.

It is with some irony that the *Born to Fail?* study refers to another report, more than half a century earlier, by the Edwardian economic historian and social critic R H Tawney[2], which had itself suggested, 'The continuance of social evils is not due to the fact that we do not know what is right, but that we prefer to continue doing what is wrong. Those who have the power to remove them do not have the will, and those who have the will have not, as yet, the power.'

Born to Fail? challenged readers who'd discovered in its pages what life was like for children like me and my sister Susan to think about what their 'will' could be.

> Do we want technological progress, or human progress? Are we more interested in a bigger national cake so that some children get a bigger slice eventually – or are we ready for disadvantaged children to have a bigger slice now, even if as a result our personal slice is smaller?

Crucially it challenged its readers to ask if they cared about children born to fail and asserted, in its final page, that:

> If children are indeed our country's investment in the future, then everyone has a stake in their welfare.

Of course, my peers and I had no idea of any of this when we were being asked questions by teachers who took us aside at school or health visitors who came to our homes. We'd be squeezed into the last decent dresses that fitted and given a Ribena carton to hold before they arrived so we could answer 'yes' to the predictable 'have you had a drink today?' question. And I had even less of an idea that my work, 59 years on, would be addressing these same issues in a new but often not very different world.

But here I am, at this crucial time in our history, wanting to reflect on the questions asked nearly 50 years ago in that report, which are shockingly (worryingly) still relevant decades later. To examine what we consider to be the working class and our current aspirations for social mobility and what they mean to each other – or could mean.

I am an educationist, a working class Professor, and my work – my personal, moral purpose – is to help establish a system that ensures all children are given the chance to achieve and to make sure they all have choices to secure decent work and a safe home; ultimately to enhance their life chances. I believe this is a human right – for all families to have the health and wellbeing they and their children deserve.

At the time of writing, one in six children are living in poverty in the UK: a shocking 2.5 million children. Alongside this statistic is the newest report from the Social Mobility Commission[3], 'Time to Change', which underlines that we have a social mobility problem that is getting worse for a generation of young people and that the most disadvantaged pupils in England have fallen even further behind their peers in their schooling. And according to the Education Policy Institute (EPI)[4] the most disadvantaged youngsters in England (those who have been eligible for free school meals for at least 80 per cent of their time in school) are, on average, more than two full years of learning behind non-disadvantaged pupils by the end of secondary school. The Education Policy Institute point out that – despite investment and targeted intervention programmes by the Government – that gap for the persistently disadvantaged youngsters has widened rather than closed in the last ten years. While the gap is closing slightly for other groups, that improvement is slow and inconsistent, says the EPI report. For example, from 2007 to 2016, the gap by the end of primary school for disadvantaged pupils had narrowed just 2.8 months in the nine years. At the current rate of progress, the EPI assert it would take a full 50 years to reach an equitable education system where disadvantaged pupils did not fall behind during formal education to age 16.

This is, I believe, a terrible indictment of the supposed progress of the last half century.

How can this have happened?

As I travel around the UK with my work it is increasingly apparent to me that there are whole communities where there is little or no aspiration or hope. Bleak places where people don't seem to have space to breathe and where children are disadvantaged before they are born.

The issue here is intergenerational and the need to break the cycle is self-evident. Families are desperate for change, desperate for a solution. They want an effective alternative way and I can see that this is where businesses, charities and political leaders can join together to engage new thinking and action. They need leaders with a clear moral purpose who are prepared to invest time and resources, creating authentic partnerships that can develop aspiration and hope – a sense of 'can do'.

Social mobility involves changing the way people think, act and engage. To understand that there is an alternative way to live, that everyone can succeed. We need to act fast; we need to galvanise society to act against what is ultimately the social injustice of our time.

The business of education is clearly crucial to change. But education cannot be considered in isolation if we – as a society that believes in social justice – are going to rise to the challenge and do something about this. It's clear that unless we start thinking in a joined-up way, we will not be able to move forward as fast and as effectively as we need to.

What does this joined-up thinking mean? It means conserving the interdependence of housing, education, the judicial and prison systems and policies relating to school exclusions and young people not in employment, education and training (NEET) and examining the impact of that on family life.

Instead, we tend to consider these factors in isolation. This silo mentality in our society has left the health service overwhelmed with the problems they have to treat, the prison service building bigger prisons to meet demand, social housing in neglect, and those in education also left to feel overwhelmed by having to meet the targets of traditional teaching while addressing a much wider remit – supporting children who feel anxious and invisible and who are the victims of poverty. The enormous human cost aside, we're seeing from a societal perspective how a failure to properly tackle our social mobility problem and the attainment gaps entrenched in the education system is an extraordinary waste of human capital, and an unnecessary cost to the taxpayer.

As a result, too many of those teachers, unable to see how change will come and feeling helpless, are abandoning their profession. The latest school workforce census data released in June 2017[5], shows ongoing problems with teacher recruitment and retention. In 2016 we saw the lowest entry rate for teachers in five years – and, at the same time, people are leaving the profession faster than ever. This, says the report, leaves 600,000 pupils in England taught by unqualified teachers and we know that the schools who struggle most to recruit teachers are those teaching disadvantaged children. In 2017 – as pupils returned to school – there were warnings from politicians[6] of schools being on 'the verge of a major crisis' and Professor John Howson, an expert on the school labour market, was reporting on the final set of Universities and Colleges Admissions Service numbers for students joining teacher training courses and concluded schools will find it harder to recruit teachers in 2018 than at the time of writing in 2017.[7]

So why are we still failing to see the connections? Why aren't we looking at better ways to spend the millions we pour into recruitment and training to replace the lost expertise?

The Social Mobility Commission[8] has called on the Government to invest in a ten-year plan with targets that are monitored. This includes considerable investment in early years (redirecting money spent on wealthy older people); the development of the whole child rather than exam results in schools; an increase of apprenticeships for young people rather than adult workers; and engagement and improvement of parenting rather than a reliance on moving from welfare to work. And David Laws, Executive Chairman of the Education Policy Institute, has called for a focus on improved teacher training to match some of the best OECD countries and economies.[9]

The call for action is fundamentally welcomed. Perhaps it will inspire a more positive and proactive narrative about the future, so we can learn from our failures as well as from those ideas that have been successful. There is hope. In my work around the country I've seen how changes in thinking patterns can have extraordinary results; results that challenge the injustice of disadvantage, and that underline our need to listen. That's what led me to write this book.

Chapter 2
Is this just a matter for the working class?

I have seen and been motivated by some great work on social mobility throughout my career and clearly, for some time, an improvement of social mobility has been lagging behind so much public policy. There have been some, if clearly not enough, positive social outcomes from individual initiatives and now there are new ones on the table, happily ensuring this conversation continues. Some of these, indeed, are directly in response to the aforementioned Time for Change assessment. In a speech at the Sutton Trust's Social Mobility Summit 2017[10], the Secretary of State for Education, Justine Greening, spoke of a 'social mobility emergency' and the need to focus on 'cold spot' areas of Britain and 'the most entrenched forms of disadvantage'. She asked, 'Why should living in one area, growing up in one area, disadvantage you, when compared to another? It shouldn't, but in this country, it still does.' She spoke of the need for an effort across education, businesses and communities. And she told business leaders that the country can only rise to the challenge of developing the skills and talents of our young people if Government and business work together.

I was born ten years after Aneurin Bevan's 'healthcare for all' NHS[11] was founded, and just as the service's first vaccination scheme was launched. I experienced the earliest attempts at comprehensive education in the late 60s and 70s. If I look back over my life it has been punctuated by the launch of reforms and initiatives in the education arena: for example the growth of further education; the outlawing of corporal punishment in state-funded schools in 1986[12] (I had my fair share of the slipper in advance of that); the raising of the school leaving age to 16 (1972)[13] and then, in 2008, to 18[14]; the launch of Sure Start in 1999; the Pupil Premium in 2011[15], and, in 2014, the biggest round of Special Educational Needs and Disability (SEND) reforms[16, 17] since the Warnock Report in 1978[18] in a bid to reach those children with SEND more effectively. These were all underpinned by a desire to promote equality and social mobility; to ensure we harness the talents of young people for the future. The initiators of every one of those reforms shared the belief that every single young person has talents we should value.

I look back at my childhood and while it's taken me a long time to unpack all the literal and metaphorical boxes from that time, I can see how we surely benefited from many of those initiatives. And some might conclude that I, a class migrant by all accounts, am a sort of proof that hard work and aspiration supported by appropriate social policy can lift people out of deprivation – a testament to the meritocracy of our society.

In fact, I would beg to differ. There are far too many people who, like me, experienced disadvantage in the 70s and who didn't succeed. We all know huge swathes of the population who, even today, still get nowhere, in spite of their talents, commitment, aspiration and the hard work they do. The idea that social mobility depends on personal drive and the will to succeed is a tempting one for people in power, but in reality it is much more complicated than that. Indeed, it's dangerous – because it shifts the responsibility of social mobility onto the individual, when often that individual is not in any position to something about it. It is vital for Governments and bodies to avoid this sentiment.

The current notion, for example, that A Levels are accessible to all is difficult to follow. We know that only one third of 16-year-olds move onto this stage of study and that those following vocational courses instead are often criticised for not taking a more academic route, even if it would have little or no bearing on their future. I've witnessed many examples of young people faced with the dilemma of retaking exams or stopping education when faced with school and society's expectation that they'd continue to university. I've also witnessed young people step off the academic route and achieve huge success. My own brother went straight from school into a position as a trainee butcher, at 18 becoming one of the youngest managers, and by 21 earning accreditation as a master butcher. He is now a very successful businessman. There are, of course, many people sitting on Boards of hugely successful companies in the UK who started off stacking shelves or on the shop floor and bypassed university altogether, but they are rarely held up as an example of what can be done in a way that shapes social mobility policy.

A study by the Centre for Global Higher Education at the University College London Institute for Education recently highlighted these inequalities (in access to higher education, graduation from higher education and economic success post-graduation). It pointed out that further education colleges – more likely to offer vocational qualifications – account for 8.5 per cent of higher education students but were at risk of being ignored in policy discussions which focused on getting disadvantaged students to selective universities.[19]

The reality is that not all universities accept vocational qualifications, limiting the options available to disadvantaged 18-year-olds. This is compounded by the negative rhetoric on the value of Btec qualifications[20], which are more accessible to vulnerable and disadvantaged students.

A secondary headteacher and colleague recently recounted how students from two neighbouring schools had been refused entry into year 12 (post 16), due to the mix of their year 11 results, which were more focused on vocational than academic courses. His school was only one of two in his densely populated area to have open access to post-16 study.

Meanwhile I meet young people every day who disrupt their study for exams, or re-sits of exams, with hours of application forms and days travelling to interviews if they manage to get one, and who continue to find it amounts to nothing. Often, they don't even get an acknowledgement from the company they want to work for, let alone feedback they might find useful. I see people from all walks of life, including those who work in school, giving 60 hours a week to try and make their corner of the world better, whilst feeling undervalued and overworked and not listened to. I meet people who've spent years going from one low paid job to the next – often struggling in between short-term contracts – living with no security, rising housing costs, and no opportunity to get the work experience and skills they need to climb out of poverty.

If it was all about rewarding effort, we'd be having a very different conversation and our country would be in a very different shape.

But I have learned a great deal in my journey to now. About the power of individual teachers to create a sense of self belief – the 'I CAN' our children today so badly need. About the random kindness of strangers and how it can guide our path. About the role of housing and health, the justice system and the teaching profession that shapes our education sector and which has shaped my thinking and beliefs.

I am a great believer that, given the opportunity, we can improve what is happening in schools, and by working across sectors – housing, health, charity, business – we can create opportunities, better opportunities, for young people when they leave.

Defined by class?

When I was growing up the working class were defined by their family background, housing, work and income. The most widely validated measure of social class, the Nuffield or Goldthorpe class scheme[21], was developed in the 70s while I was at the local comprehensive school. It placed people in one of seven main classes according to their occupation and employment status and was more rigorous than its predecessors, distinguishing between people working in routine or semi-routine occupations employed on a 'labour contract' on the one hand, and those working in professional or managerial occupations employed on a 'service contract' on the other. Based on my experience in the lowest class, it didn't, though, capture the role of social and cultural processes in generating class divisions.

More recently there was the huge BBC Great British Class Survey[22], which was launched in 2011 (and published in 2013) and based on 160,000 responses, making it one of the UK's largest ever studies of class. It was, as well, unusually detailed in its questions about social, cultural and economic capital and also suggested that people in the UK fit into seven social classes. But it claimed that the previous definition according to occupation, wealth and education was too simplistic, and brought in economic, social and cultural dimensions. In the new definition there is a technical middle class (prosperous in terms of income, but scoring low for social and cultural capital), new affluent workers (social and culturally active with middling levels of capital), traditional working class (scoring low on all capital but not completely deprived and with reasonably high house values), emergent service workers (a new, urban group which is relatively poor financially but has high social and cultural capital), and the precarious proletariat – the poorest and most deprived.

While this was heralded as a way to get a more complete picture of class in modern Britain, and the ideas that came out of it seemed exciting (i.e., a new affluent worker class which included children of the traditional working class), we should not take our eye off the most central question – namely, how fair is it across the board or across those classifications when it comes to health, education and housing? How much choice do we give people either to stay and enjoy where they are and what they've got, or to explore new areas of work or learning? How can we get to the stage where every individual, whatever their class, has value – and are themselves valuable to us all?

Dr John Goldthorpe, a sociologist at the University of Oxford whose team developed the aforementioned Goldthorpe class scheme, suggested in the British Academy Sociology lecture in 2016[23] that little has changed in society since World War II; largely because more advantaged families are using their economic, social and cultural advantage to ensure their children stay at the top of the social class ladder. He also argued that the reforms designed to increase access to education haven't had the impact on social mobility we had hoped to see. 'A situation is emerging that is quite new in modern British history,' he says. 'Young people entering the labour market today face far less favourable mobility prospects than their parents – or grandparents.'

And he argues that 'what can be achieved through educational policy alone is limited – far more so than politicians find it convenient to suppose. To look to the educational system itself to provide a solution to the problem of inequality of opportunity is to impose an undue burden on it. Rather, a whole range of economic and social policies is needed."

The idea that as a working class person you are going to fail is a betrayal: a blatantly wrong assumption. But the other betrayal is the idea that there will ever be equality. Equality of income, status or housing. Society has already determined that this is not possible. Some of our policies have championed the deceit of a classless Britain and we would be wise – as we make decisions that will determine what kind of social mobility report we'll be reading about in another 10 years – to be more honest about the motivation behind these policies, and what is realistically the way to improve social mobility.

We would also be wise to recognise that social mobility shouldn't be seen as migrating to a different class, but about life chances for everyone. Equality of opportunity and value. Opportunity for education, to secure the skills to work, and a job to meet your needs. Equality to make choices (which depends on people being able to see what else is available to them and to be free to seek out the education, skills or work to get there). A recognition that everyone has something to offer and every individual is a valuable part of the society we live in and where there is a sense of mutuality: our worth to each other and our value in supporting, if not fighting, for each other. When that's in place we might get policies that recognise and are built around the idea that by helping one sector of the population it helps us all. We might start to look at a society – and to build a society – where everyone has choices, to improve things for themselves where they are, or to improve things for themselves by moving away.

Chapter 3
What does social mobility really mean?

I am always uncomfortable with what seems to me a national obsession with rating the social mobility of a family by the numbers who get to university, rescued by the middle-class ideal of what it means to have a successful life. Successful people who are class migrants are often described (as I have been) as the first in their family to make the break when they secure a place to study after school. Obviously, the numbers heading to university are important. The fact that for every child attending university from families in the lowest 40 per cent income bracket, seven do not; the fact that just four out of 100 Gypsy, Roma and Irish traveler pupils manage to access higher education, and the latest figures which showed only 1 in 5 people in parts of the North West (Knowsley) progressed to university compared to 1 in 2 in parts of Buckinghamshire, are worrying examples of limited social mobility.[24]

Furthermore, a report from the Office for Fair Access (Offa)[25] recently commented[26] that the proportion of young people from poorer families who do not continue after their first year has reached its highest level for five years, with nearly one in five leaving their course before their second year. Offa's director Professor Les Ebdon called for further, faster change, and rightly pointed out that it wasn't just about getting in, but about getting on and relayed his concerns that universities are not doing enough to support students from different backgrounds when they get to university.[27]

I believe we should make sure we don't react to figures by looking at higher education as the only measure of success or assume it guarantees upward social mobility. In the aforementioned report by Teach First, for example, young people from the poorest backgrounds are believed to be constantly held back by social mobility hurdles which their wealthier peers do not face. The report asks if the £725m universities spent in England on measures to help disadvantaged students get to university in 2015-2016 could be spent more effectively, earlier on and in harder-to-reach communities – including schemes to encourage aspiration in the early years and primary phases, through partnerships with parents and carers.[28]

I also welcomed the latest report from Reform this year – 'Joining the elite: how top universities can enhance social mobility'[29] – which explored how the most selective universities can diversify their intake of students. The report ranks the 29 highest-tariff English higher education institutions according to their progress in admitting more disadvantaged students and, again, we see improvements have been remarkably slow. Crucially it questions the investment, suggesting there is a lack of understanding where funding (in 2015-16, more than a billion pounds) is invested and how its effectiveness is measured. The report recommends that higher education institutions should report spending in greater detail, to allow for assessments of whether they are achieving value for money.

I come back to the thinking that measures of academic success are misplaced if we do not recognise the multiple issues faced by the working class: the most fundamental is the ability to find a job to secure a safe place to live. We too easily overlook that, I believe, because we too often judge someone's social or cultural capital by a middle class view of what is acceptable. This might well be reflected in the underfunding and reform of post-16 education, which increases the focus on academic success and takes it off less academic skills. In his recent column in the *Times Educational Supplement*[30,] Geoff Barton, general secretary of the Association of School and College Leaders, took up the causes and the case of limited curriculum, writing: 'The Government talks about social justice. But the underfunding and reform of post-16 education undermines the arts and languages in state schools and colleges, and takes away the kind of supportive AS structure that helps young people from less academic backgrounds.'

In agreement with Geoff, this way of thinking is the opposite, in my view, to the mutuality I believe in. Let's take sport, music and art as an example. They are great levelers, and good for everyone, but the caveat is that they can only do so if you have access to them, and can enjoy them in a way that suits you and your life. They can be about being on a local football team or going to Wimbledon, about listening to iTunes or going to a festival, about a pop concert or the Proms. Value judgments about what is a good way to spend your time are subjective and unhelpful.

Through this lens we can be more honest about the barriers to social mobility and more open to ideas about how we break them down. More honest about how we can make life better for everyone, rather than focusing on policies that aim to rescue the talented or the worthy from one sector of society and find them a place in another.

When people talk about their working class background they are often criticised for getting romantic about poverty when they know as I know that there is nothing romantic about it. What they are doing, more often than not, is asking us to look at the value of social networks, the social camaraderie, the tribal element of the traditional working class and to respect that, value it and learn from it, when we look at how we can make a difference to people who are part of that network.

I am not advocating that no one migrates from one class to another. I know how important it is to avoid any rose-tinted view of working class life – life sitting in cold rooms, or the 'security' of jobs that were often monotonous and back-breaking but which barely secured food on the table and a new school uniform in September. My dad was bad and sad and my mum was depressed, both products of their own desperate upbringings. My brother had been sent away to live with my dad's cousin in Canada and my sister Susan and I grew up being told and believing that to ensure we had clothes on our back and shoes on our feet and food on the table we'd have to work to pay for it. We worked at Woolworths to start with. Too short to serve behind the counter we were given the job of changing old money labels into new ones; this was February 1971 when my sister and I were 12 and it was the time of decimalisation. To get myself promoted, I saved up and purchased impossibly high platform shoes so I'd be moved to work behind the sweet counter. On Sundays I'd be sent to tidy up a dentist's garden and there were long evenings turning spools of wool into neat balls for shop sale, or into ponchos (my sister crocheted) for my mum to sell. Or we would thread spring bars into mountainous piles of watch straps (my mother did piecework for a local watch factory). Much of that money was siphoned off by my dad, who was addicted to drink.

But throughout this time, I did see and feel the value in the social networks around us, the tribal element of extended family, in our case in the form of neighbours in our street. The other mums who'd look out for ours, the teacher down the road who taught us to read, and the woman behind the counter at Woolworths who helped us get that job.

I hear colleagues – in education and social care – surprised when visiting housing estates filled with families in the direst need, discovering not only a community that knows each other but a community that really cares. They are surprised because they have often visited with trepidation. When my charity works with parents and carers in schools – including those who seem least likely to engage and so the hardest to reach – we usually discover families who can teach us a lot about how we can reach their children more effectively and who want more than anything to make life better for their children, despite any false start on our side, or fear of schools on theirs.

We should never ignore families – parents and carers, as I'll explore later, have a crucial role to play in helping us promote social mobility – or the communities they come from which give growing children a sense of their value to their neighbours and to each other, and later to the workplace. We can see examples of the good that comes out of those communities every day if we look hard enough. Search out Radio 4's *Listening Project*[31] from the 50-year-old Branholme Estate in Hull, which has been through the toughest times since it was built to solve the post-war housing crisis in the city. Today community leaders speak movingly about how people who have very little materially give vast amounts to each other every day. And how, despite seeing cuts decimate 10 years of good work, they witness daily how people do amazing things with opportunities when given them. Consider how the community around Grenfell Tower responded so vividly after the fire, or how older employees in a Port Talbot steel company took a reduction in their pensions to allow for future investment and to keep work coming for the generation that followed them. Or look in areas of poverty all over the country where the communities have, to others' shame I'd suggest, embraced immigrants and refugees in ways I don't see so regularly where I now live in the Home Counties.

We're also starting to hear more and more from employers, that when they recruit they are looking for people who haven't just got their eye on the top of the career ladder, but who want to make a difference to the community where the company or organisation is based. In fact, I know of employers actively seeking out those *without* university degrees so they can train and progress them to deliver those values and the work ethic that some graduates they interview don't have.

We need to make sure initiatives responding to this trend are not only promoted as opportunities to support social mobility, but promoted in a fair way. There are good examples of organisations, who have open access to apprenticeships, as opposed to those, (the majority), who now require standard level qualifications (five subjects at grade 4 or above, or 5 A*–C). The latter simply perpetuates a system that creates barriers for at least one third of the population.

For those students who want to progress to university, degree apprenticeships (launched by the Government in 2015)[32] could fit well into the model, allowing students to learn as they earn, studying while in employment with their tuition fees were covered. But in this arena, too, those from disadvantaged backgrounds are – it seems – not enjoying fair access, when courses aimed at widening participation are at risk of serving the middle class elite. The Chartered Management Institute reports that their survey[33] showed school leavers from disadvantaged backgrounds are at risk of missing out on 'free' degree apprenticeships – affluent parents being 2.5 times more likely than less well-off families to know about this route to university. Their Director of Strategy, Petra Wilson commenting: 'We're now in danger of higher apprenticeships quickly transforming from being perceived as an alternative route into employment for the less able, to being a highly attractive option out of reach to all but the elite. Universities, schools and employers need to work with parents to raise awareness, challenge perceptions and help all young people to consider this new route to a degree and employment.'

Working class solidarities and values have been under attack by unemployment, low pay and recent recessions (particularly resulting in the closure of factories and ship yards and collieries replaced by short term, zero hours contracts at the lowest levels of pay on or below the minimum wage), but they have survived in many parts of our country. The professional classes know, if they're honest, that their own working life rarely creates that collective cohesion and commonality.

It's a subject explored expertly in two American books on the working class. Joan C Williams's *White Working Class*[34] suggests we've misunderstood class issues in the Trump and Brexit era, either assuming working class is the same as 'poor', or assuming working class people want to join the upper-middle class. Instead Williams asserts they may simply want to stay true to their own values in their own communities, but with the security of a job, fair pay and a decent home. At the same time J D Vance's brilliant *Hillbilly Elegy*[35] sees him wishing he didn't have to leave his community and family to better himself, and recognising it was that same extended family, friends and local teachers who all helped give him the chance to do just that. Aware of all the studies on resilience, Vance says he knows life changed for him when he moved in with his grandmother and had the security of a loving home. When he was, quite simply, happy. When people around him – in his community and later in the Marines – gave him a sense that he had choices, and that his choices mattered.

It might be convenient for some people to avoid the class issue, but if we do so we can't have a conversation about how to make Britain fairer for everyone, or how we can all benefit, and all be enriched by real social mobility and the mutual benefits it affords. The barriers we need to square up to are not so much about (and certainly not only about) the still-stifled numbers who can make it to university. More, they are about the numbers who feel valued to get a job and a home and who can access the education – good education and vocational training – they need for both.

Why can't we not only utilise families but give them what they need – the housing, social care and education where their family is – which would then give them the choices to move if that's right for them? I recently worked with a family at a school who were trying to get housing near work they'd been promised and a school that could support their child with special needs. Every single layer of the application required a reference, and a charge (some as high as £200) for the agency to get that reference once they'd been given the name and address. These things were not relevant to the work or effort they were putting in to improve their lot. And worse, might easily have landed them in that vicious circle of despair where they could not see a way out. All because of something as simple (and in this case ineffectual) as a housing application.

Instead of taking children out of their homes, their communities (or making parents move house and home to seek better education), why not improve it where they are? Analysis of Ofsted data by Teach First[36] shows that at the moment only 15 per cent of children from the poorest 30 per cent of families attend a primary school rated by Ofsted as outstanding, compared with 27 per cent of children from the richest 30 per cent of families. More than one in ten children from the poorest families attend a primary school rated as inadequate or requiring improvement (Ofsted's two lowest tiers) compared with around 1 in 16 of children from the richest households. The percentage of poorest children going onto a secondary school rated as inadequate or requiring improvement by Ofsted is 24 per cent, compared to 10 per cent from wealthier families.

My journey to now

The reason I decided to go into education was because it was all I knew. It was not about having a menu of choices as a result of my comprehensive education. Schools I went to delivered the curriculum they were familiar with, dependent on the staffing and the ambitions of leaders from the lowest levels of the three-tier system (secondary modern, technical and grammar). In those days, my sister and I spent hours of our school week learning to wash, repair and iron jumpers. The only professional people I knew were doctors, dentists, nurses or teachers – and I happen to be the most squeamish person on the planet when it comes to anything medical. As it happily turned out, education is a good and satisfying place for me to be.

Teachers were also the people who had shown the most kindness to me. Like a teacher called Gerald Hall who played the double bass in various dance bands and cinemas in the 40s and 50s and came to teach brass instruments to children in my school. He wasn't qualified, but it was thanks to him that Susan and I got two cornets. Despite the fact that they were battered and over-used, we loved them. My dad would go ballistic if we played at home and for a while confiscated the instruments to the loft. We retrieved them, hiding in a cupboard to practice, and when he threw us out we would find a quiet corner to play outside, or – if it was raining – climb into the back of his car to carry on.

Then there was a mentor, a technical drawing teacher and gifted musician called Richard Scholar, a pivotal figure in my past (he won't acknowledge it, despite my ongoing thanks). He launched a school band and a local brass band and let us play in them. That took me out of our estate to perform and gave my sister and me our first experience of being part of something bigger than ourselves, and to be applauded for our success. From there I talked my way into the music group at school, teaching myself guitar chords so I could accompany a performance of *Joseph and the Amazing Technicolor Dreamcoat* as well as joining my sister to play the fanfares for Pharaoh's entrance on my cornet.

There was also a light bulb moment for me around this time when I cashed in our stash of Green Shield stamps for a soft toy – my mum was poorly again and loved soft toys so I'd gone to the shops to choose one. I had the sense that exams were like the stamps – if I collected a few results, I might be able to cash them in for a better job. I'd failed all my exams at school but went home, slightly euphoric, and persuaded my mum that I shouldn't leave school but should stay on and re-sit.

It took me five goes to get my English qualification. My English teacher had long given up on me ever getting it – every school report evidences this. We had no books in the house growing up, and I read my first proper book – Jane Austen's *Emma* – at 15.

But the re-sits eventually won me a place at Bretton Hall College in Yorkshire to study music and it was there that a college tutor called Harold Dabbs, perhaps seeing my work ethic and ambition, pointed out that my voice was going to hold me back. My strong, if lazy west London accent was barely understood by my tutors in Yorkshire and Mr Dabbs suggested that until I became understandable, I wouldn't get a job. He prescribed me endless Sunday newspapers and supplements to improve my vocabulary, and – as the college delivered drama as well as music – he arranged elocution lessons, not to make me posh but to help me pronounce words properly. It worked. When I graduated I got a job teaching music and went on to study for a Masters in Music Education at Reading University. When I graduated my father gave me one last thrashing. It was not the first time he'd hit me, but it was the last. It left me with no desire to join the celebratory drinks party that came after. I remember, too, that when I'd been studying at college I'd invited my parents to see me conducting a college production of Gilbert and Sullivan's *The Mikado*. They commented, all too loudly, on my need to stand on a bathroom stool in the orchestra pit (I was only just over 5ft), perhaps seeing it as a symbol of me trying to be above my station. In fact, they seemed more fascinated by my need to stand on a stool than my achievement in conducting a 100-piece ensemble.

So, no, I never wear rose-tinted glasses about a life of hardship or a life polluted by addiction or mental health issues. But I did hear cutting through my own story the confusion and discomfort my family felt with the idea that to get on you had to get out and turn your back on where you come from. Perhaps my mum and dad thought I was denying who I was and trying to be something I wasn't.

And perhaps, it strikes me sometimes in my work now, that's what we (as in the middle class professional generation) aspire for others – to make them more like us, and maybe that goes some way to explain why real social mobility isn't happening.

Time to listen

I am pretty confident that most politicians, regardless of ideological stance, go into the profession to make a positive difference. But when things haven't worked, there can appear to be a reluctance to accept that and learn from it. Instead of the long-term solutions we need, there can be a temptation to go for visual, public-pleasing quick fixes that might make those in the professional classes feel more comfortable but don't really solve things in the long term for any of us. And, more importantly, there seems to be a reluctance to listen, and really hear the voices of the people they are trying to help.

That keeps coming through loud and clear, most notably when the failure to listen impacts on the whole country and not just those doing the shouting. We've seen hard evidence of that since the Grenfell Tower fire in 2017, too long after the residents had been calling for improvements to safety in their homes.

As the 2017 Social Mobility Commission report[37] points out, 'The public mood is sour, sometimes angry. Whole tracts of Britain feel left behind. Whole communities feel the benefits of globalisation have passed them by. Whole sections of society feel they are not getting a fair chance to succeed.'

Lisa McKenzie writing in *The Guardian*[38] after the Brexit vote suggested the working class were sick of being called ignorant or racist because of their valid concerns, and the EU referendum gave them their chance to have their say and opened up a Pandora's Box of working class anger. She lives in working class communities, researches and writes about them as a working class academic and in this article suggested the EU referendum had become a referendum on almost everything of working class concern. While immigration was part of the debate (and many reports blamed racism for the working class vote), it was actually more about housing, schools and wages; about fears for elderly parents and what happens if the rent goes up. She pointed out that in Nottinghamshire even former striking miners were voting to leave, worried about the lack of secure work and the rising problem of poverty in their communities. They saw the referendum as a chance to have their say, and McKenzie suggests they were, collectively, saying that things are worse, not better, than they used to be. That this was about the precariousness of being working class, when people's basic needs are no longer secure. 'The referendum has opened up a chasm of inequality in the UK and the monsters of a deeply divided and unfair society are crawling out.'

Later, Jonathan Freedland[39] writing in the same paper after the Grenfell Tower fire in 2017 pointed out that the tragedy marked a point of no return. That the fire was a story of 'inequality, of the poor herded into a cramped building made unsafe because it was prettified to improve the view of the nearby rich.'

What these and other commentators are rightly calling for is an understanding that no decision can be made – in housing or healthcare or education – without input from the people on the ground who are supposed to benefit from it. This is where mutuality wins – when people work together to say what is needed, rather than one section of the population (too often the professional classes), deciding what should be prescribed for another section of the population, and worse, without giving them the chance to contribute.

Once we've recognised the strength of families and the communities we want so much to improve, we can utilise those strengths to help make those improvements, so we can give people a choice to stay or to move on according to individual ambitions or life plans – one not necessarily being better than the other.

I've also seen the extraordinary success that comes not from 'rescuing' people like me from those situations, but from making those situations better so we have choices. In education recent notable success stories have come out of Sure Start[40] and the Pupil Premium[41], work with SEND reforms[42] (those with SEND are more likely to come from less advantaged family circumstances) and indeed our own pilot research at Achievement for All[43], giving schools the resources to reach out and relate to pupils in new ways; or create units run like extended families, giving parents, carers and children a place and an opportunity to improve things for themselves and each other.

Pupil premium funding, for example, is enabling schools to effectively address the learning challenges faced by disadvantaged pupils. Since it was introduced in April 2011, more and more schools are using the funding effectively to raise the attainment of their less advantaged pupils. Sharples *et al* (2011) in their review[44] highlighted, for example, rigorous monitoring of pupil data, parental engagement, the development of high aspirations and supporting school transition. Ofsted (2013) in their report on successful use of Pupil Premium[45] underlined how effective schools ringfenced funding, drew on research evidence of what works, allocated the best teachers to intervention groups, trained support staff, provided pupils with clear feedback, involved governors and rigorously monitored and evaluated impact.

The same success can be seen in many early years settings like Sure Start with extended opportunities for parent and carer education; they are a haven of peace, and a place where families can open up about the challenges they're facing. In that atmosphere of trust and mutual respect, they can learn more (through the inbuilt adult education the good ones offer) so they can enhance not only their own lives, but also support their children more effectively as they enhance theirs. Go into a successful one and there is a sense of community celebration that speaks to me more than anything else about the social mobility and social justice we really want to see.

Chapter 4
Why does mutuality matter?

If we are in a place and at a time when there has to be a new way of thinking, there has to be both a recognition of the great things that have come out of initiatives (in health, social care, and education), and indeed, recognise what hasn't worked and what isn't working. Rather than repeating mistakes, or exacerbating them, have a will to change. That will have to come from both sides, and is about mutual gain.

Mutual gain happens when people, on all sides of the political spectrum, and across all classes and cultures, own the change and have a role to play. We've seen how it can work. In 2007, we stopped smoking in public places. Within a few years we saw the rate of childhood hospital admissions for asthma reversed and a drop in heart attack emergency admissions[46]. Go back further and the change was seat belts, made compulsory in 1982 and now we all wear them, without complaint. They reduced the risk of death by 45 per cent and the risk of serious injury by 50 per cent. Wearing a seatbelt now saves over 2,000 lives a year.[47]

Or consider cot death. When researchers discovered that children were less likely to die from Sudden Infant Death Syndrome (SIDS

– it was an epidemic between 1970 and 1991) by being put to sleep on their back instead of their front, the Back to Sleep campaign had a remarkable public health benefit, reducing the rate of SIDS by 85 per cent[48]. These are policies that work because everyone owns the change – everyone has a will to get behind it and feels the benefits.

So how would it work in education, if everyone saw and owned the benefits of social mobility across class and community? And what difference would it make to the working class and their social mobility?

What is mutuality?

Perhaps it's easiest to start by saying what mutuality isn't. It isn't pouring money into certain areas of the country without asking the people who live there how they'd like to see money spent – without properly exploring what they need, rather than what others decide they need. And it isn't about reshaping those areas in the image of the people giving the money. Nor is it about telling everyone they should get better exam results and aim for university. Actually, it includes resisting the urge to make those numbers a test of our social mobility.

Instead, mutuality is about ensuring everyone has the chance to read, write and engage in maths so they have choices – about what they learn, and what they do with that learning. That might be to learn more by going to university, or it might be to learn a trade or to travel the world. Mutuality is about schools and a curriculum that is relevant to their lives and which engages with them, so they can engage with larger society – it isn't a 'social distributor of life chances', as the 1973 *Born to Fail?* study claims.

We know that when children and young people don't achieve what they're capable of achieving, it has a long-term legacy effect on society. This is estimated to cost the UK economy some £77 billion a year. In 2014, 120,000 13-year-olds were at risk of becoming NEETs; this group 'collectively stand to lose £6.4 billion over their lifetimes'.[49] These are young people we risk losing track of completely. Extending the school leaving age to 18 has only served to relocate the problem that was experienced at 16 and many who now struggle to stay in education – re-sitting exams and losing what little confidence they have left – are at a pivotal age when questions about the future are dominant.

Whereas, if all children and young people facing economic disadvantage received high-quality early education the gap in achievement could be closed by between 20-50%.[50]

Mutuality is not middle class professional people dipping their toe into a life of disadvantage and then going away feeling they understand enough to call the shots. Mutuality is giving the other party a voice so they can engage – in a long-term way – on what happens next by working in partnership with others.

Mutuality isn't about rescuing people. It's about valuing them and allowing them to develop in their own way, where they are now, or where they want to be. Mutuality is, I believe, social justice and the key to social mobility.

As I moved through teaching, and then onto the wider world of educational practice, I've been able to take my childhood experience and to hold onto what it taught me. I am astonished, all this time later, that I still meet children like me who are considered born to fail. And I still meet teachers – good, hard working professionals, overwhelmed and undervalued – who are on their way to hating their job and giving up because they haven't had the right support to give these children the chance to achieve.

But I've also learned – via the schools I work in and the teachers I work with – that we can change that. I see it every day. Schools –

some in the most difficult of environments – can embrace change in really exciting ways. This teaches me and teaches us all what social mobility could really look like for everyone in the future. Those schools have taught me about the things that matter.

Chapter 5
Can we build social mobility` from the inside?

Over the last six years I've been involved in a programme that has reached nearly four million children and young people, their families and teaching professionals in a bid to support not only what they do but also change the way we think about education and its outcomes. Crucially I've learned from that work how important it is we focus on core strength, building social mobility from the inside.

When the Prime Minister Teresa May addressed social mobility in her 2016 'Britain, the great meritocracy speech'[51] she rightly talked about the need to think differently about what disadvantage means and the complex nature of disadvantage. But behind the desire for a so-called meritocracy 'where talent and hard work' matter, there needs to be more debate about how we help children realise their talents in the first place. Beyond the need for the 'successful policies such as a renewed focus on learning the basics of reading in primary schools' and 'initiatives to help young people pursue a strong academic core of subjects at secondary level' to ensure 'every child has the opportunity to develop the core knowledge that underpins everything else' there is a need, first, to develop *core strength*.

Core strength in this context is the confidence and ability to learn, develop and participate in society and it has to be understood and built in the earliest years, and be nourished as children grow. It's clear that children and young people experiencing disadvantage and underachievement lack confidence. They find learning challenging, they develop differently and they may ultimately have limited participation in society. Underlying factors, or needs, may be cognitive, physical, emotional or social; each are manifest in a fundamental lack of progress of the child or young person when compared to their peers.

While initiatives and interventions can be bespoke there is a danger that we focus entirely on one group when we talk about social mobility in schools. Of course, studies have rightly highlighted that there are groups which demand our attention. We know, for example, that white working class boys' poor performance at GCSE level (only 24 per cent gain five A*–Cs) makes them the lowest or second-lowest ethnic group over the past decade[52]. We also know that low-income families start off behind other families in our communities and risk never catching up. In the latter example this starts with early years development – problems with speech, language, play and so learning. And then the gap actually increases so by the time they get to Key Stage 2 at least one in four of those children born into low-income families has difficulty learning, particularly around literacy and numeracy. The gap increases as they go onwards to Key Stage 4.

But to make a difference to any group (age, class, or ethnic group) we should – I believe – focus on everyone, and at every age. Not second-guessing the problems they may face, judging or classifying in a negligent manner, or assuming those same problems are confined to one group of children. Meaningful change in society will only occur if we invest in all children and young people, find what is great inside them, dig it out and share it with the world.

This is an exciting time to be in education, albeit a sometimes stressful one. The work of the Sutton Trust and a host of relevant organisations is focusing hearts and minds on the challenge ahead. We're seeing projects – like the Europe wide Raising the Achievement of All Learners in Inclusive Education project[53] – recognise the high cost of school failure and inequity for individuals. Projects like this one, and more besides, are bringing policy makers together with parents, school leaders and learners to look at what teaching approaches can be most effective in raising attainment and contributing to the now urgent conversation about how we look afresh at social mobility in a meaningful way. We need to find the will inside ourselves to drive a change based on mutuality so we enrich the lives of the children who most need help in a way that enriches the life of every child in the school, and the communities where they live.

Greater expectations

I am not naive about the challenges we face and the needs of the children coming into schools. Analysis by the Education Policy Institute (EPI)[54] found that children defined as 'persistently disadvantaged', (those who are entitled to free school meals for 80 per cent of their time at secondary school) are, on average, more than two years behind their peers in terms of academic achievement by the end of secondary school. The study also found that while progress has been made in narrowing the attainment gap for 'disadvantaged' pupils (defined as those who are entitled to Pupil Premium funding), it warns that this gap is closing 'slowly and inconsistently' – despite considerable investment and targeted intervention programmes by the Government.

However, I do believe causality is often misinterpreted as a definitive diagnosis – and this is rooted in a deficit model. In other words, children and young people are defined by 'they can't do this because they have a problem'. This leads to labelling, low expectations, and rhetoric of failure. That's a state of being that is no good for parents and carers or teachers or for the children in their care.

Teachers who've reached these children, however, have discovered in a myriad of joyous, satisfying and career-defining ways that these children can succeed. They know these children might be dogged by adults' low expectations and aspirations – including their own parents and carers – and they may be less likely to have books at home, the space to do homework, or a parent or carer with the time to help. They know they are less likely to have access to private dance, drama, music or sport coaching, the stuff that can build confidence and friendships.

But while they have recognised the need, and the risks, and indeed elements that *can't* be changed they have also seen what *can* be changed for those children – alterable issues and alternative ways. They've also seen how they – as teachers – can change their own behaviours, embrace new ideas, or develop their own practice to provide a window on that alternative. Part of the change is simply to allow for an alternative, and to see what alternative means. I have recently seen the experience of a family with six boys whose mother realised her low expectations were holding them back and who was supported by her children's teacher as she embarked on a programme to improve her literacy. As direct consequence her middle four boys moved from being on the SEND register. Their mother's motivation and raised self- esteem and confidence were reflected onto her children, and her youngest has just started school with the highest expectations, loving the fact his mum is chair of the school PTA.

We need to look harder at studies illustrating what's possible. Like the example highlighted in the recent report by Save the Children[55] which suggested that those children who attend a nursery with a highly qualified member of staff are almost 10 per cent more likely to reach the expected level of development by the time they start school. Although the number of settings employing a member of staff with Early Years Teacher Status is increasing, many do not have this.

Or a study in maths at primary level by the Fair Educational Alliance, Achievement for All and KPMG.[56] We know that children from socio-economic disadvantage are more likely to underachieve in maths throughout their career. But strong maths skills and understanding at age 11 provide a basis for success at secondary school and beyond. As the report states, in 2016 just over half of all children from disadvantaged families achieved the expected level in maths at age 11 (58 per cent) compared to 76 per cent of their more advantaged peers. Despite this need for improvement, the study did show how schools (including schools in the most disadvantaged areas) are closing that attainment gap. In general, it was about having a whole school approach. Within that, specific ideas were working, like an enterprise week across the school, ensuring those likely to underachieve were exposed to the same maths-rich experience as their peers, or pre-lesson sessions for some pupils to go over a concept they'd failed to grasp in a previous class, or maths workshops for parents and carers to help them support learning at home.

There is other exciting work looking at the role of mentoring in secondary schools. Early in 2016 the Government put out a call for evidence, seeking the feedback of young people, their parents, and professionals in the healthcare and educational arena about their experiences with mentoring. One comprehensive school[57]

I've worked with saw their scheme not only increase attendance at school and with extra-curricular activities, but also enhance academic attainment. Students who were identified as struggling made, on average, an incredible 1.7 years of reading age progress in six weeks. The impact of greater expectations in this context is not just academic but rounded in its approach. 'It astounded us,' said the assistant head. 'But making this group of children feel happy and confident to come to school by providing them with mentors simply elevated their ability to make progress. And we have the results to prove that every year.'

Respecting parents and carers

This mentoring project was, as it happens, the result of parent feedback. The school on the Wirral had tried academic interventions but felt they were still not making the difference they wanted to see. It was during conversations with parents and carers of the target group of pupils that the issue of friendships and social struggles was raised, and instead of being dismissed (as parents concerns about social struggles often are) the mentoring project was born, and the school has never looked back.

This is a good point to address the myth that good parenting is a one-size-fits-all concept and think of parents as part of this inclusive thinking. Of course, when it comes to supporting the working classes, it's the size that fits the middle class that is usually the one people are supposed to aspire to. We talk about single parents, or unemployed parents, or low incomes as if that in itself suggests bad parenting and it doesn't – these situations are circumstantial.

What if we were to suggest that no way is right or wrong, and that all types of parenting can bring benefits, and all types of parenting requires support. This would allow parent communities to work together, for each other, in a truly mutually beneficial way and for those in education to look more effectively at the specific barriers facing children who are looked after, or children who live with grandparents or children from single parent families or indeed children from families where both work long hours.

We know that parents are the first and most enduring educators of their child (Desforges, C. And Abouchaar, A., 2003)[58] and how they bring up their child at home matters more than their income, job or situation. The good news is that this means that there is something that can be done in the earliest years to break this cycle of a poor start leading to poor outcomes. Trying to fix the challenges parents face individually may seem impossible, but we've seen – with parents as with children – that there are alterable issues, needs that can be met for the good of the whole family. If we focus on these (while working to improve housing and social care) then change can come.

The Social Mobility Commission[59] recommends a new parental support package at key transition points in family life including helping parents if the child's two-year-old check shows they are falling behind. Whilst this is probably a good idea, it is hard to see how having a team swoop in like this will help a parent who already lacks confidence and feels like a failure and now has it publicly revealed for all to see and comment on.

But other recent investment in parenting programmes has seen some success, particularly when those programmes are presented as a positive thing, with no stigma attached for those accessing them. After all, if the role of the parent is so central to the child's future outcomes, isn't it short-sighted to take the approach that only some parents need parenting classes, and to cut funding down? Wouldn't it be much better to acknowledge the importance of parenting and look at what parents need and want – to try to create a society that doesn't stigmatise parents who need to be equal partners in any development that impacts on their family? It would make more sense to engage parents and carers in conversations about how school and home can work together. I was once asked by a journalist during a radio interview why it was important to include parents in the education of children. The context of the question was news of a school who'd locked the gate to parents, allowing dialogue with teachers only after an appointment had been made by phone. The situation had reached a point where children attending the school were simply experiencing two cultures. One where teachers did not respect parents, and the other where parents did not respect teachers – a situation that was not only hugely unhelpful (if not devastating) for the children, but also for the community.

Teachers tell me that where they work in schools with a large number of vulnerable, young, unsupported parents, those parents want to make a better life for themselves. When schools offer non-stigmatised support – via training or mentoring or group classes that embrace the idea of early health assessments – the parents embrace it and look to tackle issues like housing or debt head-on. Many schools I now work in partnership with, (including one that has its own school-based Citizens Advice Bureau[60]), offer facilities for parents and carers to sort out social issues, with support. If nothing else, they give a warm welcome, a cup of tea and access to phones and computers. Children's centres who work with parents and carers in a respectful, inclusive way, offering adult education in a bid to improve those parents' employment prospects and their ability to support their children through school, see a high uptake of these facilities.

At Achievement for All the role of the parent or carer in supporting the child's education and therefore their educational outcome is held in the highest regard. We take a different approach to the traditional 'information giving' or 'done to' classes. Firstly, parents and carers are considered to be experts in the subject of their child and they are respected as their child's first and most enduring educators. Secondly, Achievement for All train and support key people in settings to develop strong respectful partnerships with those parents and carers based on the individual needs of the child. This begins with 'Achieving Early'[61], where the key person is trained then uses a structured conversation called 'Taking Time for Talk' to engage parents and carers in their child's learning. Training and support are also provided in related programmes at school and further education phases.

Rather than telling families what they should be doing, they work with the parents and carers to support them with how their child is learning and how they can support them at home. Families find this empowering as they are actively involved in the process and encouraged to contribute their ideas. The results have been astonishing, with even the most reluctant-to-engage parents (sometimes referred as 'hard to reach') making positive changes to their own parenting as a result, and raising aspirations for their children as they move forward. Teachers talk about a buzz in the school as they discover new ways to reach children, and new partners in parents who want to help them do just that.

To achieve universal change, including engaging parents and carers of the most vulnerable and disadvantaged (Lamb Inquiry, 2009)[62], coaching is needed for professionals, parents and carers. The Social Mobility Commission[63] have highlighted the need for this support to be free and with complementary on-line support. Online classes require a level of literacy, and a level of motivation not held by all parents and carers. High-impact, evidence-based programmes are in place in a limited number of disadvantaged areas.[64,65]

A new approach to aspirations, access, attainment and achievement

Teachers know the power of aspiration, the 'I CAN', and how a culture of high expectations for all children – every child, every day, every lesson in every week – can make a difference. But some children and their families are too quickly labelled as having low aspirations and not surprisingly then become the low achieving.

These children need to be given the understanding that they can achieve. We need to foster and nurture that belief. This 'I CAN' is a sense of self belief that enables them to reflect on themselves in a positive, meaningful way. It's a development of that grit and resilience that makes them persevere, and helps them understand that learning, thinking and achieving is for them.

In contrast to other commentators, I don't see aspiration as the child or young person thinking about what they are going to do when they leave school (though that can be a fun part of it), and it's not about the child or young person thinking they are going to be the best dancer, or the best footballer. Aspiration is about the here and now.

For this to happen we need children to access the 'I DO', the participation that makes learning real and which helps them become independent learners. Teachers need – and most want – to understand what the barriers are for children and how they can be removed. Not the barriers outside their remit (they can and should be tackled in tandem by appropriate bodies in a socially just society), but those in the classroom. Teachers who have seen mutuality in action – where every child is included – see the whole class benefiting from a calmer, kinder and more inclusive atmosphere.

Removing the barriers can be quite straightforward, like a child not having a pencil or a pen, or coming into school without their protractor or book. Why do we spend time – precious learning time – focusing on what they haven't got, instead of focusing on what they have got: time, in the classroom, with a teacher?

It could also be something as simple as the way we greet children who struggle to come in and who arrive late or are frequently absent. What positive impact will a scolding do as they arrive in reception and again, later, in front of their peers when they arrive in class? Is that going to help them learn, or help anyone else in the class learn? When I work in schools that have taken a step back and rethought their policy, I've seen receptionists trained to welcome and reassure those who struggle, and/or a mentor assigned to help these children into class. It's a small thing, but it can completely change that child's experience and help them focus in lessons, which can then promote kindness and inclusion across the class.

Or it may involve a new approach in the staff room. I've been in too many where staff sit silently, shaking their heads about their last class. But I've been in others where teachers have their heads together sharing their problems and ideas for how to solve them, teaming up to take classes with new teachers or those colleagues who've come unstuck. In one staff room there was a display chart of target children on the wall, covered in Post-It notes as the whole school team (from head teacher through to lunchtime assistant) shared observations and ideas that might make life better for individual pupils. Ideas that had come from staff who didn't think they had a say, or who weren't responsible for the child but wanted to help.

Teachers can support this way of thinking by reaching out to specialist charities. There are scores ready and willing to share their expertise via training, from the National Society for the Prevention of Cruelty to Children to the National Autistic Society. Carers Trust[66], for example, have done some astonishing work helping schools identify and support young carers (and there are hundreds of thousands of children who help care for a disabled sibling or support a parent suffering from physical or mental health problems) and create an ethos where they and their families – who might be embarrassed to share what's going on at home – are respected and valued and so able to talk about the child's caring responsibilities. In its Young Adult Carers at School Survey[67] the Trust found that more than four in ten young carers had no one particular adult at school who recognised them as a carer, or who helped them as a result. But once they were recognised, the charity says simple things like flexibility about arrival times, or the chance to use the phone at lunchtime, or homework support in schools, made the biggest difference. They were suffering needlessly before because of 'the rules', by making some basic allowances, pupils' work improved enormously.

The I DO also refers to activities outside the classroom, which have to be part of the culture of the school and the learning and give all children the chance to enrich their lives with extracurricular activities. When Achievement for All team up with a school leadership team we always ask them what they do with the children's free time, and request an audit of who stays on for after-school clubs, or which families attend school socials. Many teams who had assumed everything was all right, or that issues under the spotlight weren't related to specific groups of pupils, quickly realised via the audit how few students with SEND or those on free school meals or LAC (looked after children) or other pupils with specific challenges show up at these extracurricular activities. Indeed, sometimes none do; and it becomes very clear how few pupils who are under-achieving for whatever reason are there after school.

The surveys and audits we do at Achievement for All demonstrate over and over that pupils with low confidence are not only less likely to attend extracurricular activities in or out of school, but are also more likely to be absent or late, don't have a strong circle of friends and are less likely to attend parties or weekend/after-school socials with their peers. As a result they are less happy and so often have difficulty concentrating in class.

This isn't about saying to pupils 'you have to sign up to a club' or 'you must come to every school social' or even saying to friends 'you must play with girl A or boy B.' It is subtler and also way smarter than that. It's about asking children, all children, and their families what would work for them, and creating activities – tried and tested and supervised – to help children develop strengths and friendships outside the classroom and so build their confidence when they go back in. Schools tell me that once they start to model inclusive behaviour in this way, children model it too. Those children – the ones who are achieving well and don't seem to face barriers to learning – again build their own emotional intelligence as they become part of a wider community, which values and supports everyone in it.

We apply the same rule to playtimes and lunchtimes when we work in schools. Many leadership teams see these 15- or 30-minute breaks as a chance for staff to take a breather and for children to develop social skills through play, but perhaps don't fully appreciate that for those children who struggle socially, or don't have social skills to develop, or who are learning anti-social behaviours from those around them, these breaks are negatively impacting on what happens when they go back into class.

In schools, the I DO can be about a whole range of other interventions. Breakfast and lunch provision, a new more substantive trained learning role for the Teaching Assistant (TA)[68], or a mix of bespoke initiatives which can seem small but can lead to significant change. I've seen the lunchtime Lego Club that taught children with social and communication problems how to connect and build friendships. The father who was taught to read so he could support his daughter (he's now a TA). Or the child who was nurtured by the school gardener, allowed to work outside each morning, and was taught maths as he planted bulbs and fixed fences until his confidence grew greater than his school phobia and he joined his class inside. Or the 14-year-old, on his fourth school in two years, whose mum explained his passion for IT with a listening teacher, and who was embraced by the head of the IT department and given the chance to make a video about the school. For the first time, he felt valued and valuable to his community. He's now doing his A Levels. The work of the Youth Sport Trust[69] provides so many good examples. Their Team Leader programme (which trains pupils to lead and manage and mentor sports teams) has illustrated brilliantly how sport – and in particular working with and leading teams – can give pupils confidence that they can take back into class.

These children moved from the 'I CAN' to the 'I DO' to the 'I HAVE'; the 'I HAVE' being the opportunity to consider all that they have learned, reflecting on the processes that will take them where they want to go, like a springboard to further progress.

The initiatives that took them from the 'I CAN' to the 'I HAVE' are all things we *can* do or issues we *can* alter for children in our care right now. All things which can help close that attainment gap. And the result when they achieve is the 'I AM', that feel good factor that results from the internalization of learning and success, equipping children and young people to understand what they know and how to learn and a desire to engage with a future educational journey.

A boy I met in a Pupil Referral Unit in 2012 when filming a clip for Achievement for All described his journey:

Waking up one day, the word 'achieve' kept coming back to me, I CAN achieve! I was told that there was a possibility of going back to mainstream schools. Up until then I wasn't someone who was nice to know, not someone you would like to meet in the street. I worked hard, doing my work and thinking about exams (I DO). The first exam was not what I thought it would be, I passed (I HAVE)! Not something I would have thought about a year ago. I know what I want to do now, I am going to Art College, my mum is really proud, and so am I. I want to get a job in graphic design, my mate's dad knows someone… (I AM).

The benefits I've seen, one child at a time, one school after another, are greater than the sum of all the stories I could tell you. The focus on what might be altered rather than what couldn't be changed supported everything else these great schools were trying to do and properly utilised the stunning teaching skills they have.

Chapter 6
Why make teaching challenging?

Teachers opt for their profession because they want to work with children, and to change the lives of children. The best places to do that are, of course, early years settings, schools and colleges. We know that as part of an education system we can have a profound and positive impact on lives – that we are temporary but important stewards on a child's journey, and their experiences while in our care can and do shape what happens next. Not just in terms of the grades they get or the college offers they receive or the career they end up in, but in terms of their feelings of self-worth, their sense of place in their class, their community and thus in the wider world. As well, of course, as in their behaviour towards others and in the relationships they form (or don't form) as they reach adulthood.

As teachers we know that the stories we read in the paper each day about disengaged young people falling into the most frightening of situations underline the need to reach children early, to ensure they leave school not only with qualifications and a future plan, but with confidence and self-worth. And yet many teachers – way too many – know that youngsters in their school can and do slip through the net. Not because they don't care, or don't want to help these pupils, but because they are in a school where leaders are stressing about the return of Ofsted inspectors, or there's discontent among staff or they are firefighting underachievement or behaviour problems with interventions that separate pupils rather than bring them together. It has, as a result, become accepted by some that a large proportion of the school won't achieve; that this proportion will leave without the confidence or qualifications to secure a future where they can progress.

Where does that leave us, the teachers? Over-stressed? Under-valued? With little sense of professional satisfaction? It's not a coincidence that record numbers are leaving the profession early on in their career or mid-career, feeling isolated and burnt out. But it is one of the most urgent problems in education today.

It is, of course, of little surprise to many in education. Teachers today are too often coming out of college with the curious belief that they should somehow know everything when they are in front of a class. This is something that has both emerged from and subsequently fed a culture of fear and stress in the profession, with teachers saying they feel judged rather than supported by their professional peers (be it fellow teachers coming into the staff room or Ofsted coming in to inspect). They see parents and carers as people who complain about rather than collaborate with them, and see neighbouring schools as competition rather than a source of inspiration which could, via co-operation, support families across their local community. It's this culture that causes too many teachers either to give up their job or to struggle on demotivated, bemoaning their fate, the state of the system and the fortunes of the children around them.

We need to ask ourselves why we have fallen into this trap. Why should we think we know it all when we get so little time being trained to look at special needs, the impact of being fostered or adopted, the role of young carers, the symptoms of undiagnosed dyslexia, or the impact of bullying? Why do we come into an education system that is supposed to be inclusive, and into a classroom designed to cater for a whole raft of children with a whole range of needs and abilities – and decide we should know it all? Why, if we've taught children with dyslexia or autism or Attention Deficit Hyperactivity Disorder (ADHD) in one year do we automatically expect to understand and reach children in the next (who probably present in very different ways), without the help of experts, including the child's parents or carers? And why, whenever new changes come in do we feel overwhelmed by them, and believe we are being over-monitored and messed about?

This is something we can change, if we have the will to do so. Most teachers I speak to see the value of breakfast and lunch – I believe it should be given to every child every day. But it shouldn't be the job of the teachers to prepare and deliver it instead of working with children and preparing lessons. And as cuts increase across the education service, that's something that can happen. Teachers I work with are seeing the huge and lasting benefits of working with parents, but they need a family liaison team to forge those links, so teachers can sit down and work with them for the benefit of their teaching and the child. They know that mental health must be prioritised as a matter of urgency, but know they don't have mandatory mental health training when they see problems they can feel powerless to help.

It's here in schools, and now as the crisis worsens, that we need to think outside the box about everything from funding to the curriculum to ongoing continuing professional training. Increasingly teachers are considered to be the resource for resolving all the challenges children bring into the class. Rather than debating who gets free breakfasts or whether it should be lunch instead, having a non-teaching support team who provide both for everyone would make a difference to the school as a community, including the teachers who have to support children who are tired and hungry and so unable to learn. Rather than training teachers to become mental health specialists, having a counsellor in situ, supporting the teachers by supporting those pupils with emotional difficulties – that might be as a result of a caring role or a family crisis, bullying or bereavement – would prevent problems escalating and instead promote a culture of kindness and support that would only enhance learning. Rather than requiring teachers to literally paper over the cracks, having schools that are well maintained – that sparkle and shine – so staff, children and the wider community can take pride in them would create a more positive culture.

Could these initiatives, I dare to suggest, pay for themselves by saving the money spent replacing those teachers leaving the profession, or the growing price tag of mental health problems?

It worries me that large sums of money are poured into certain schemes and projects that have very little evidence-based impact. In some cases, these schemes perpetuate the divide that already exists. A recent report from the Education Endowment Foundation[70] stated that a random controlled testing trial of a joint project involving Teach First, Future Leaders and Teaching Leaders failed to demonstrate any impact on pupil progress when compared to other non-participating schools. Of course, this is only part of the Teach First and Future Leaders story, both were created to address teacher and leadership shortages across England and any programmes that improve teacher and leadership recruitment should be applauded. Teach First is a significant recruiter of graduates and career changers, having enhanced the status of initial teacher training through the development of a unique approach to leadership and teaching. I am proud of having created and implemented the Ofsted-rated outstanding Teach First initial teacher training programme whilst Dean (and later Pro-Vice Chancellor) at Canterbury Christ Church University. I am also proud of every graduate of the programme who has remained in the profession, many of them in working class areas, and how the programme's been developed since, including the approach to recruitment developed by the award-winning James Darley and his team. Teach First is now established as a major contributor to teacher recruitment alongside other university led collaborations with schools, providing a teaching resource for the most disadvantaged communities across England and Wales. Funding for all teacher training programmes continues to be subject to review. As a member of the All Party Parliamentary Group for the Future of Teaching I am a firm advocate of a mixed economy in the initial teacher training sector, encouraging a range of graduates and career changers into the profession through a range of courses.

However, initial teacher training is exactly what it says on the tin, 'initial training'. The importance of continuing professional development for all of the profession is self-evident. Support and development is available in all major professions covering law, medicine, accountancy and more, but the position of continuing professional development in teaching is dire. Since the introduction of Baker Days in the 1980s there has been little monitoring of impact on practice of in service education and training (INSET) for teachers, and little to show for the billions of pounds invested in evidence light programmes delivered in the name of school improvement. EPI found that if we continue to approach pupil progress investing in under researched programmes there will be little or no improvement.[71]

Retention of teachers is an urgent, national issue – more so in challenging communities. We know the number of teachers leaving the profession is greater than the number entering and a recent survey (of 3000 members aged 35 and under) by the teachers' union, the NUT, found 45 per cent said they intended to leave the profession within five years, 85 per cent identifying 'volume of workload' with 45 per cent citing 'mental health concerns' as opposed to pay. Nearly three quarters said they were working over 50 hours a week.[72]

Meanwhile the LKMco 'Why Teach?' Report in 2016[73] revealed that teachers primarily go into the profession to make a difference and are overwhelmed by meaningless workload. More than three out of four teachers who've considered leaving the profession have done so because of workload. If the product (the teaching itself) is not right, people won't of course stay in the profession, and others won't join. Let's not forget that for the most part, the need to recruit is the flip side of a failure to retain.

Being a beginner teacher is a professionally challenging role in any school. In schools in areas facing socio-economic disadvantage these challenges can be multiplied exponentially. This means that the retention of teachers is poorest in areas of disadvantage; the very areas where the need for continuity of teaching and the use of cutting-edge proven teaching strategies is needed the most (see Cordingley *et al*, 2014[74]). Almost 50,000 teachers in England left the profession in 2014. This equates to one in 10 teachers leaving the profession – the highest for 10 years, and an increase of more than 25 per cent over five years. The stress and difficulty of working as a beginner teacher means that they are especially likely to leave teaching.[75]

To address this fundamental problem, The Cornwall College Group, the Institute of Education and Edge Hill University joined forces to create the RETAIN project[76], funded by the Education Endowment

Foundation. The RETAIN pilot (2016-2017) provides relevant and focused professional development support to beginner teachers in disadvantaged coastal towns in Cornwall. RETAIN supports beginner teachers to understand the impact of disadvantage, to understand and use teaching approaches that overturns that impact, and to plan their own career progression. This creates a virtuous circle where children and young people facing disadvantage benefit from relevant high-quality teaching, and beginner teachers are supported to remain in the profession and develop further their skills and capacities, providing ever-increasing quality teaching and increasing their own career satisfaction.

At the time of writing, the pilot RETAIN project is being independently evaluated by Sheffield Hallam University. Early indicators from the module evaluations suggest that RETAIN is having a positive impact on both the outcomes for children and young people, and the future retention of teachers.

But there are other examples – key ones that support teachers' wellbeing and effectiveness – that are held back because of lack of learning (about their results) and the funding that should be invested.

Everyone knows mental health is a problem we have to address in schools and, as above, is cited by some teachers as the cause of their wanting to leave the profession. Figures suggest rates of depression and anxiety among teenagers have increased by 70 per cent in the past 25 years[77] and one in ten children and young people (aged 5–16) suffer from a diagnosable mental health disorder and as many as one in 15 children and young people deliberately self-harm.[78] Some 55 per cent of children who have been bullied develop depression as adults.[79] While school leaders and politicians are recognising tackling this issue must be a priority, projects that are making a difference are not always given the funding they need.

Place2Be, the charity that provides considerable expertise and a counselling service in schools[80], has shown that 73 per cent of the children they reach who have severe difficulties improve after counselling. Sixty-two per cent improve in their learning, and 79 per cent say friendships are better. In any one year they currently deliver a remarkable 65,000 sessions, so this is a huge number of people being reached and helped. This is not only down to it being right where children need it each day, every day, but also as a result of the multilayered service – counsellors get the support of a clinical team and expert advice. They know, too, that all children benefit as a result, not just those referred to the counselling. This is the case not only in classes without distractions (75 per cent of children who go to counselling are less disruptive) but crucially by the generation of an atmosphere that promotes emotional wellbeing. The charity also offers a support network for teachers; a place to think and talk through the difficulties they are dealing with in class.

The charity's own economic analysis has found that every pound spent on this early intervention creates a return of £6 in savings to society. Think what that kind of service could achieve if it was in thousands, instead of hundreds, of schools.

Let's look at another example. Since 2011, more than £9 billion has been invested by the Government into Pupil Premiums (as mentioned in Chapter 4)[81], with great effect in some schools and early years settings. Currently around two million pupils attract this support each year. However, while there has been improvement in attainment at Key Stage 2 and 4, the gap remains. There have been calls, (for example, Professor Stephen Gorard in 2017[82]), to improve this by building on what evidence shows is working. In the case of Pupil Premiums this would be, for example, the use of the funding for leaders with a strong vision, ring fencing funding, drawing on research evidence of what works, allocating the best teachers to intervention groups, training support staff, rigorous monitoring of pupil data, parental engagement, developing high aspirations, supporting school transition, addressing social and emotional competencies, providing pupils with clear feedback, ensuring all teachers know which pupils were eligible for funding, providing support for attendance, involving governors and rigorously monitoring and evaluating impact.

In the context of early years, the Social Mobility Commission has recommended increasing Pupil Premium investment in early years by 100 per cent. Take a setting with 15 eligible children, additional income is £4,531.50. Doubling the money would increase this to £9,063. How would we justify this additional investment? Well – for every £1 spent on early years education, £7 must be spent to have the same impact in adolescence, according to Public Health England 2015.[83] And if we supported this resource with more training, and extended the Early Years Pupil Premium to include two-year-olds, with all spending monitored against impact – the effects could be even greater.

In addition, I would suggest that whenever we launch a new idea, the starting point should be an understanding of the needs of the community (not our own analysis of the needs), and a mapped-out, short-, medium- and long-term evaluation. Not necessarily randomised control trials, (measuring impact of an intervention in an experimental setting compared to a similar non-experimental setting over a set period), but qualitative research that gives us a greater understanding of how people can work together. It is the reality of the classroom that thousands of interactions that take place in every lesson are fundamental to understanding pedagogy.

New measures of success

If we are to embrace new ideas, raise our expectations of and aspirations for children, and really give teachers the support they need to do their job, I'd also suggest we have to have new measures of success that move beyond academic knowledge and which have the potential to embrace social and cultural challenges experienced by the working class. While quantitative analysis has a place in assessing the start and end point, what happens in between is descriptive, empirical and lived, and really values the profession of the school staff. Too often and too easily, the initiatives that many see working in their community or school are cut or changed or challenged because they don't meet someone else's criteria for success. In schools we know this can be those hallowed exam grades carving a path to university, and a reversion to that idea that it's the best if not only measure of social mobility.

In his latest study, 'What Predicts a Successful Life? A Life-course Model of Wellbeing'[84],Professor Richard Layard and his team at the London School of Economics' Centre for Economic Performance have concluded that a child's emotional health is far more important to their satisfaction levels as an adult than other factors (including academic success when young or wealth when older), another challenge to the assumption that academic achievement matters more than anything else. It was interesting, too, to see one of the most shared teacher blogs post 2017 GCSE results relating to a boy who'd triumphed by getting two Fs in his GCSEs[85], his special school headteacher Jarlath O'Brien arguing that the child in question had overcome phenomenal challenges to get into and stay in school, and demonstrated life changing positive behavior change while sticking to his studies as a result of the commitment of school staff and the support of his mum. Most would agree that we need to hear more about students like this every summer.

While grades are important, there are a myriad of measurements of success. Decision makers should listen hard to teachers as they talk about attendance and the disadvantaged – meaning that children want to be in school, and their families recognise its value. Some heads feel huge success if their children – who may be new to the country, or have been through trauma – are smiling at the end of the day, or feel able to approach them (or their staff) when they have an issue. Others celebrate the lunchtime club that has fostered friendships for children who'd felt isolated, or the books children discovered and loved to read. Or teachers can simply remember the day when pupils discovered a talent or a passion for something new.

Campaigns and initiatives driving these less celebrated outcomes may not get as much attention or the levels of funding seen elsewhere, but they are equally important in promoting success and – in turn – helping support those grades schools are after. I can trace my own desire to get on to the discovery of books and a love of reading. I see now how the 'Read On. Get On.' campaign[86], led by a coalition of charities, works to challenge head on the fact that a fifth of all children in England, and close to a third of the poorest children, are unable to read when they leave school – a crucial contributing factor in the educational divide.

I have found that learning and the area it covers can be a way to communicate with a family, and with individuals in it. If relevant it can empower them to get a job, to open a bank account and manage a budget and secure a home. Of course, algebra and languages and Shakespeare are important and I'd never suggest for a minute that we shouldn't be teaching and enjoying them and celebrating them. My timetable at school is an example of the limitation of a prescribed curriculum. I resented having to spend hour after hour in my school learning how to wash, repair and iron sweaters – the unspoken message being that, as a working class pupil in a working class community this was a skill that would be central to my future happiness. This isn't about patronising families, but about understanding them, and understanding what is relevant (or not) to their lives at the outset so they can meet their basic needs and, crucially, have choices about where life takes them next. The introduction of the national curriculum in 1988[87] changed teaching and opened up the possibility that every child could access the same knowledge, skills and understanding in every subject. What was missing at this point was an understanding of social and cultural relevance.

Regardless of background, challenge and need, achievements come in a variety of forms, and in all avenues of life. We know and celebrate this in the successful middle-class arenas without question – I've met many a successful professional who'll confess to having hated university and discovered his or her talent in a new area of work. Or who has given up what everyone else thought was a successful career to start a new business, or to downsize and live a simpler life. Or who've failed at their dream but found a better route to something they love. And I've met people my age who've resisted university all their life and suddenly decided to study at The Open University to learn something new and wonderful. Nobody questions the wisdom of that, or the right of the individual to decide themselves. The ability and capacity to make choices is a fundamental right.

But do working class children have the same opportunities to make choices? I don't think so. Everyone in education understands Maslow's five-tier hierarchy of needs[88], and the need to meet lower level needs (food, warmth, security *etc*) and emotional needs (like friendship, that provide a sense of belonging) before focusing on the next set of needs – esteem and a feeling of accomplishment, which are, of course, the prerequisite to self-actualisation when we can fulfil our potential. While everybody wants to move up the hierarchy, progress is hampered or stalled by a failure to meet those lower level needs.

Education must acknowledge and understand children's basic needs and work (if necessary with other partner organisations) to try to meet them if it is to make a difference and allow them to enjoy a sense of their own self-worth and progress to carve out the kind of life they want, where they want to live it – moving forward to become a better version of themselves. Isn't that everybody's aspiration, every day?

Recognising that, we need to think as we put today's curriculum together where we want it to take us. Instead of focusing on the big world where the same work is supposedly open to everyone, could we start closer to the actual places people live in, where they can extend through learning and language and experience? In schools where I have worked I've seen the hardest-to-reach children tune in and engage when teachers relate learning to their individual passions. Those might be gardening or running, computer games or fishing, building or basketball, music or the media. I've seen how, when nurtured and understood in a way that involves them, teachers can give those young people confidence in themselves and so a desire to learn more. That is core strength, and building social mobility from the inside out. But it depends on their needs being recognized, their talents being identified and their potential talents being spotted, embraced and encouraged.

Yet I've seen this kind of learning squeezed off the timetable. And to what cost? Every year some 35 per cent of children never appear in the much-lauded results. In the UK, we like to see that 66 per cent achieved grades A*–C (or the now newly graded 4–9) without ever wondering what happened to the other 34 per cent. In an average large secondary school, that can be up to 100 pupils each year whose choices have, too often, simply been taken away.

We hear a lot about equal opportunities but in the context of social mobility you can only have them if there is the opportunity to be equal. To learn, to work, to live. There is plenty of evidence of the attainment gap in Britain, but no evidence that it cannot be closed for all children, regardless of background, challenge and need. That should give us hope, and a will and desire to change.

Rethinking exclusions

As I write, yet more research about the impact of exclusion from school has been published, this time from the University of Exeter[89] highlighting how it can lead to pupils developing a range of disorders, including anxiety, depression and behavioural problems. In other recent reports about exclusion statistics[90] a significant increase in figures was reported. Almost 6,700 children were permanently excluded from primary, secondary and special schools in 2015/16 – around 35 each day. The report argued that this rise could be blamed on children becoming disengaged from school as the curriculum narrowed, and focused on testing, especially among the youngest children. The teachers quoted also warned about the impact of cuts to the number of teaching assistants, who often support disruptive pupils.

If exclusions become permanent we know the impact that can have. A study by the Institute for Public Policy Research (IPPR) reports[91] that half of all pupils expelled from school are suffering from a recognised mental health problem. Those who are permanently excluded find themselves at a significant disadvantage, with only one in a hundred going on to attain five good GCSEs.

The think tank also highlights the disadvantages these children face, as those excluded are four times more likely to grow up in poverty and twice as likely to be living in care. They are also seven times more likely to have special educational needs than those who are not excluded, the report claims. After exclusion, there is a downward spiral of underachievement, with teachers in settings catering for excluded pupils twice as likely to have no educational qualifications.

As a founding trustee of the Fair Education Alliance I have been involved in the production of the 2017 Fair Education Report Card compiled by the Education Policy Institute[92]. The Report Card indicated that children from low-income families continued to be over four times as likely as other children to be permanently excluded from school, amounting to a shocking 2,580 permanent exclusions in 2014/2015. The report, produced in partnership with over 80 third sector and university organisations, found there has been a rapid rise in exclusions since 2011 with 'an extra' 300 children from low income families permanently excluded and an additional 9,000 children being on fixed term exclusions in 2014/2015 when compared to the previous year. These statistics are further evidence of the expanding divide between low income disadvantaged children and their peers.

Associate fellow of IPPR Kiran Gill is quoted[93] as saying schools felt they were pushed to exclude very challenging pupils because a lack of funding means councils are treating pupils as 'OK' unless they were excluded. 'We've spoken to head teachers who feel that excluding pupils is the only way to escalate their situation and get them support,' she said, adding that heads felt exclusion could indicate the 'severity of need' to cash-strapped councils.

Suggestions that head teachers are forced to exclude simply to get the support they need for these children must surely force us to seek out alternative solutions. And there are other solutions we must now look at, alternatives that can save young people's futures, as well as saving society a huge amount of money. In a report from Barnardo's[94], the charity provided both the quantifiable costs of exclusion to the public purse and to the individual. A place in a pupil referral unit for excluded young people (PRU) was, at the time of the report, calculated by the Government to cost £15,000 per year. The charity then investigated the costs and outcomes of running a service in the voluntary sector to reduce exclusions. Its findings were stark. Compared with the costs of exclusion, even the most intensive model of intervention saved money in the long term – as well as helping young people to resolve the issues that distract them from learning. In one of the charity's case studies, services including initiatives like a part-time vocational alternative to school, or a term-long inclusive learning programme followed by support to get back into school were found to be highly cost-effective. The cost of supporting a young person to stay in school for a year averaged at £1,696 and recorded creditable success rates in restoring young people to education. Meanwhile, the annual cost of a secondary school place is approximately £4,000. This suggests that local education authorities spent £5,696 for each of these young people to access support and retain a place at school – as opposed to the £15,000 that it would have cost for a place at a pupil referral unit, if they had been excluded.

And think of the cost to those young people who end up disengaging from society and getting caught up in crime, a story that is too common for some who are persistently excluded and costing as much as £140,000 per young person in prison each year.[95]

I have witnessed all forms of exclusion and the consequences. In addition to fixed-term and permanent exclusions internal exclusion leads to children being isolated from their peers, and developing into a sub-group within the school, which can too often be replicated outside of the school environment and risk involvement in gangs. If head teachers agree to move children between schools, it can disrupt learning further adding to the obvious feelings of rejection and isolation.

Exclusion in whatever form is unjust, unnecessary and should be removed from practice in our education system. A headteacher colleague from an inner-city school was with me at the launch of the report and, like me, had never excluded a child. We must look at alternative ways to care for these children in school, through partnerships with experts and engagement with families. Early identification of behavioural issues and there causes followed by emotional and social support are actions that prevent exclusions. I have seen how positive participation in the classroom and extracurricular activities in and out of school with the resulting sense of belonging and inevitable development of social and emotional understanding has changed behaviours in children at risk of exclusion.

As an example, low income working class and traveller children from a large primary school were given the opportunity to join a Saturday morning cycling club set up by the deputy head, and it immediately led to a significant increase in attendance and decrease in behavioural issues. The star of the club, a child from the traveller's community, is going on to represent England in cycling at junior level.

An inner-city school in the Midlands had limited space and resources, the playground fully utilised, but the deputy head never gave up on her endeavours to find the equipment (donated by a local shop) and expert coaches (*pro bono* from local club). She was determined to make a difference to the lives of those children. The impact of this action on pupil progress in the classroom was profound, as recognised by Ofsted. More importantly, the children had developed a sense of belonging, well-being, by joining in and knowing what success looked like.

Chapter 7
How can we give everyone a better start?

Everybody wants more for their own children than they had for themselves – more opportunity, more choices, or more work, whatever that work might be. But policies seem to come out of the misguided idea that we need to rescue children from their background. When those on the ground know policies should recognise and reach children where they are and make life better for them, for everyone around them. They would do this by helping them see what they can do, in a way that harnesses their talents and aspirations, even if they're not the same as ours, and which engages with their families and communities so everyone benefits. Everyone's lives are enriched as a result of social justice and the social mobility that follows – it creates a better world for us all.

There is no doubt that the first years of a child's life have a lasting impact on their life chances – by the age of five, large gaps in development have opened between children from low-income families and their better-off peers. Even more worrying is the fact that this is evident at three years of age, with a gap for cognitive outcomes of 23% between the richest and poorest children, rising to 27% by the age of five.[96] This evidence of a widening gap over time suggests that leaving it until children start school to address their cognitive development is far too late.

So how to change that? Without addressing what happens during those first five years of a child's life, we are missing a host of opportunities to address the issues surrounding social mobility. In the still relevant cross-Parliamentary report 'Seven Truths About Social Mobility, 2012'[97] MPs say giving pre-school children essential skills is the key to breaking Britain's class system and that the point of greatest leverage is between 0-3 years of age; primarily in the home.

'Good parenting and warm family relationships can make a crucial difference to a child's future prospects,' said Liberal Democrat peer Claire Tyler at the time. 'We also know from recent research that a child's emotional wellbeing, resilience and social skills matter and can affect a child's ability to bounce back from adversity.'

The contributors go on to say that the cycle can be broken through education: 'It is not that the parents' class/income directly determines outcomes for children, but rather (it) is correlated with educational attainment and it is that that drives outcomes for children.'

This is good news. Here we have two key areas – parenting and education – holding the key, recognising that change is most effective in the early years of a child's life. Finding a way of ensuring we are able to support parents and offer children high quality early education is a must if we are to break the cycle of poverty and disadvantage, and doing this in a joined-up way is surely the most logical and sensible approach.

Everyone agrees, high-quality early education has a positive impact on children's learning, development and well-being – which in turn leads to better academic, social and emotional outcomes. The Fair Education Alliance Report Cards (2015, 2016)[98] and previous Nutbrown Review (2012)[99] placed teacher quality firmly at the heart of improving outcomes for all children in early years settings. And the recent report by Save the Children, 'Untapped Potential: How England's nursery lottery is failing too many children' (2016)[100] suggests that children who attend a nursery with a highly qualified member of staff are almost 10% more likely to reach the expected level of development by the time they start school.

Although the number of early years settings employing a member of staff with Early Years Teacher Status, (and so a qualification to teach the 0–5 year age range), is increasing, many do not have this. It's a problem that is being addressed by the Government, but in the meantime, there is a lot that can be done.

What does that involve? I would argue it means developing existing practice across four areas: leadership and management; working together; progress and learning and health, and happiness and well-being.

The Achieving Early programme launched by Achievement for All in 2014[101] has worked with over 200 settings across England and Wales and supported more than 2,000 early years children who were at risk of achieving poor outcomes. In the pilot study – involving 388 children vulnerable to underachievement – the proportion of children reaching an age-appropriate level in key areas (communication and language, and personal, social and emotional development) rose by 50 per cent. Out of the 33 settings inspected during the two years of the pilot, every single one increased their grade and the programme received the Nursery World Inclusion Award 2015.[102]

Taking inclusion seriously, and making it happen

UK Government policy has promoted inclusive education since the 1978 Warnock Report[103] and it's been a global phenomenon since 1994, promoted through key practice and the fundamental philosophy of UNICEF (United Nations' Children's Fund)[104], the UNESCO Salamanca Statement on the rights of the children (1994)[105], which saw 92 Governments and 25 international organisations agree that inclusion should be the norm for children with disabilities, then later through UNESCO (United Nations Education, Science and Cultural Organisation, 2005). It is one of the keys to social mobility and yet we know that some schools have been slow on the uptake or failed to understand what inclusion means and can achieve. We have to change that, and change it quickly.

The Centre for Studies on Inclusive Education[106] outlines what inclusion involves in an educational setting. It includes the need to value all pupils equally, and to see them participating in the cultures and community of the school as well as the curricula. At its heart is acknowledgement of the barriers that stop children (all children, not just those with educational needs or disabilities) being fully involved in and learning at school and, alongside that, a determination to find ways to remove those barriers.

This all comes with a crucial commitment to utilising and valuing vulnerable students, including those identified with special educational needs and those with disabilities, as a resource to create a diverse, tolerant and inclusive school, rather than allowing them to be seen as problems to overcome. The latter can lead, too often, to a group of students withdrawn from their peers' group and taught by unqualified or the least experienced teachers. I've heard parents talking about the dozen (or more) interventions their children enjoy as a measure of the support their school is giving, without realising how much (hours and hours) they're missing out on by not being a part of the class enjoying an accessible curriculum. Needs must be picked up early and teachers trained to meet them, with a focus on outcomes. And these include wider outcomes like friendship – an undervalued but vital result – which can help children get the qualifications they need to progress confidently when they leave school.

I recognise that in our drive to see results, it can be sensible to group children who struggle into classes. However, we must ensure they don't miss out on what a more inclusive school can deliver. Schools also risk forgetting those middle attainers on SEN support as they stretch the most able on one hand and try to raise the bar for the lowest-achieving 20 per cent via special support. But then those in the middle with additional needs fail to make expected progress. At a national level, the profile of those on SEN support[107] shows that the three most common additional needs are moderate learning difficulties (27%), speech, language and communication needs (21%) and social and emotional and mental health issues (17%); additional needs are likely to overlap within these categories. Those on SEN support are also more likely to come from socio-economic disadvantage than their peers without an identified SEN and are less likely to move out of this category during their schooling.

But it does not have to be like this. An inclusive approach with frequent and rigorous interrogation of pupil data improves both progress and attainment not just for children and young people on SEN support, but also for those who aren't. This is of particular importance for those whose prior attainment is somewhere in the middle. If they fail to make the expected progress by Key Stage 2 (aged 7-11), they start secondary school behind and are less likely to 'catch up' by Key Stage 4 (aged 14-16). At 16 they move on and may not have the skills needed to gain employment or the minimum qualifications needed for further education or training. Instead, they repeat the same learning with a post-16 provider.

Ofsted is quite clear, in their review of SEND in 2010[108], that education providers who achieved the best outcomes for their pupils/students with SEN had high aspirations for their learning and focused on enabling them to become as independent as possible; this has not changed today. Getting the best outcomes for those in the middle-attaining bracket on SEN support means school leaders and teachers asking questions about their progress and attainment: what challenges do they face in learning? What challenges do they face in accessing learning? And where are the gaps? Comparisons can be made with pupils/students with similar prior attainment, using national, local and school level data sets.

The SEND reforms introduced in September 2014 have gone some way to close the gap for those on SEN support. Identification of need is more accurate and happens earlier; more teachers engage with specific professional development; and SENCOs (Special Educational Needs Coordinators), qualified to Masters Level through the National SENCO Award[109], provide the practical day-to-day guidance. But more can still be done. Until every school in England develops an inclusive approach, with teachers and leaders asking challenging questions about learning and outcomes, those on SEN support in the middle attaining band may never progress beyond that middle.

In an inclusive setting or school with an inclusive leadership all these things become part of a shared vision – those core values and beliefs which should be reflected in the school's aims and organisational practice. That vision has to be real and doable and create a sense of direction and purpose, utilising a staff's skills. The vision should not be wishful thinking on the website. It should ensure good things happen for all children.

Inclusive settings bring children – cross-class and cross-ability – together, making sure that the school itself doesn't, even if inadvertently, build barriers to social mobility by separating children or leaving them out of those activities too easily left to or dominated by the higher achievers – those theatrical or musical performances, arts displays or sporting events. Outside school we know how valuable those activities are – how every child's life can be enriched and emotional intelligence promoted by helping all children play and work together.

Children who find it difficult to play and work together with their peers are often bullied or will, unfortunately become the bully. Bullying a problem too often overlooked barrier to social mobility. Teachers still receive very little training at college on this issue and are not always clear what bullying is. Nor are they familiar with their school's anti-bullying policy or even, crucially, the impact bullying has on children's learning and long-term future. The statistics reveal a shocking picture of the problem in schools (with nearly one in three children bullied in schools) and we know those with SEND or who are in any way vulnerable are at higher risk. A study published in *The Lancet Psychiatry*[110] suggests children who are bullied at school are at even greater risk of mental health problems in later life than those who are maltreated by adults at home. The same report suggested those bullied are five times more likely to experience anxiety and twice as likely to talk of suffering depression or commit self-harm, making them even more vulnerable to a further cycle of bullying at school.

That comes at a huge cost to them, and a significant cost to us all. Children who suffer emotional and physical abuse because of how they learn, how they dress or what their parents do or where they come from can shape a view of themselves as worthless in the world around them and regard that world as something that can't be trusted and certainly not a place where they can move forward. Teachers know that if those worries are simply dismissed, children can grow up believing they should persist with relationships that are abusive, or that they shouldn't share their worries with adults. It's a problem that negatively affects everyone – the bully, the bullied and the bystanders, who are learning the same lessons and/ or feeling disempowered to act. On the other hand, children who learn they don't have to put up with abuse, and who are in a setting where it's not tolerated, build trust and friendships. And those who aren't bullied but who are encouraged to be tolerant and kind and inclusive, not only help change the lives of their peers for the better, but change their own as well by building emotional intelligence – a crucial part of their development for the future.

We have seen in society that good things happen when inclusion works properly, when all these issues are properly considered. For me, growing up, it was that chance to play in a brass band. I've seen it since working to great effect in sport, music, dance, and community groups. Groups that now recognise they can benefit not only those who face barriers to activities (including children from families on low incomes, children in care, or those excluded from school), but everyone in the group because they will all benefit from that kind of inclusion.

The end goal?

When I was growing up huge numbers of the population took a well-worn path from school to the large local employers, including manufacturers. Bear in mind that at the beginning of the 50s some 8.7 million people worked in manufacturing, compared to just 2.5 million today, and there were nearly a million in mining and quarrying (just 60,000 now). In those days, people under 25 made up one in three of the workforce, compared to one in seven today.[111]

I could go on. But we all know that today things are different.

In some ways better, more flexible, more exciting – but in many ways for many people, things are worse. My concern is that for too many young people there is no clear path, if any path at all. While the world has never been wealthier, there has – for them – never been more anxiety over work. Entry-level jobs are harder to come by – school leavers are often competing with graduates or older workers looking for employment after their own job losses. There are more persistent problems, like the low number of starter jobs that help people on the career ladder. The jobs that are there often offer less training, stability or the opportunity for growth. Or they are simply out of reach to those who haven't the qualifications or experience that's required, or the ability to survive through unpaid internships that might provide it. And if they do get a job? A recent report showed only one in four workers in low-paid jobs in 2001 went on to escape poverty and move onto higher pay.[112]

We are forever hearing people in power talking about letting people progress on their own merits, but too many people don't know what their merits are. And, if they do, they can still find it too difficult to put them to good use.

I believe in the power of education to promote social mobility, but my work in this arena has taught me that it will only happen if it is tied to real opportunity. In others words, jobs are important. They not only provide income – and so the chance to secure a home and to buy food and clothes to stay healthy – they help people connect to society around them, and benefit from a sense of their value to the community and wider world. They can, if delivered in the right way, give people the choices they need and so the capacity to change their own lives in a way that suits them. Jobs have to be a priority, and they have to shape the work we do in schools, and the support we give families outside them.

There are, happily, some great activities going on across England and

Wales now, which are aiming to build aspiration and opportunity in the heart of communities where children live, and to show them the choices they have and why those choices matter. As Joan C Williams underlines in her book *White Working Class*, elites pride themselves on merit, and point out how hard they work for what they've got. 'But so do hotel housekeepers,' she writes. 'Let's not forget that.' There are, happily, some fine discussions going on about how we treat people more fairly in the workplace, giving those low paid families and young people equal rights and opportunities to earn a decent wage and to progress as a result of their hard work. Matthew Taylor's review of working practices[113] was very welcome in its urging a rethink about the way employers treat lower paid workers, and asking them to look at strategies for lower paid sectors to ensure workers do not get stuck on that low rate of pay.

I've been into primary and secondary schools whose pupils can be third or fourth generation unemployed. But now those same schools are forging partnerships with local businesses, bringing employees and employers into schools to talk about the opportunities in their area, explaining ways children can make a difference as they grow up, and the skills – teamwork, citizenship, creativity – that children can develop as they get ready for their future. Other schools have created vocational work opportunities for their teenagers to give them an opportunity to work in an inclusive workplace, and to realise their potential value to it. Or they've developed social action programmes so they can learn how much they can contribute (and gain) by making a difference to others.

I hear from schools about cross-sector partnerships (with social care, housing, the police) so they can help each other identify risks and spot early signs and so prevent problems (homelessness, debt, neglect) that can impact so badly on a child's learning and so future prospects. I've seen big businesses working to reach out and recruit youngsters – those that have slipped through the school net – offering them a second chance to study for and re-sit qualifications while in the workplace, and while getting the work experience they need to progress at the same time. Or businesses using their older employees to mentor youngsters taking their first step onto the career ladder. In its recent Education and Skills Survey[114] the Confederation of British Industry has underlined again that we have to look harder at what skills achieve for a young person and for a business, instead of judging our educational success just on the existence of training and apprenticeships. It called for business and education to work more closely, and businesses to support schools from primary level to bring lessons to life and open up opportunities beyond the school gates. 'Across the country there are brilliant schools and colleges helping young people succeed, both academically and in terms of the attitudes and behaviours they need to succeed in later life,' says Josh Hardie, CBI Deputy Director-General. 'Business can and must do more to ensure that someone's postcode or background does not define their life chances.'

The Social Mobility Commission[115], working with the Social Mobility Foundation now ranks employers for the first time on the actions they take to ensure they are open to talent from all backgrounds. They report some great strides forward, including firms providing outreach activities and work experience and mentors. No one company had solved the problem, but the fact they were being scrutinised and scored on this is a huge step forward. It will, I hope, lead others to follow suit. Not only to benefit the youngsters who need social mobility to be prioritised, but to help themselves by making sure they don't miss out on the wealth of talent which can still so easily go to waste.

As I sign off the Government is currently creating 12 'opportunity areas' (from Derby to Hastings, Norwich to Blackpool)[116] where partnerships between early years providers, schools, colleges, universities, businesses, and organisations like the Confederation of British Industry, the National Citizen Service and the Careers and Enterprise Company will aim to draw out the talents of children in school, and to carve paths not only into universities, but into apprenticeships and entry level jobs. Each area will have a research school to support schools and lead the development of evidence-led practice.

If the leaders of the Opportunity Areas listen to and collaborate with the local community there is the possibility of improvement in these areas. Investment needs to be focused, mutually agreed and understood by all involved. There is a tendency to create activities for their own sake and spread these like confetti at a wedding, which is a short-term approach. I would advise that local working class community groups, volunteers and evidence-based activities are considered, beyond the middle class leaders who by their own circumstance will not have the depth of understanding needed to make a difference. While investment is to be applauded there is a bigger factor to be considered; Opportunity Area funding is limited to geographical areas selected by Government based on cold spots (areas of deprivation identified by education, employment and health data). At the time of writing there are at least 45 such areas in the country with many more places with more localised needs that have not been identified. The problem of improving outcomes for the disadvantaged working class is a universal one.

Chapter 8
Can we have some new thinking to answer old questions?

If anyone would have asked the 18-year-old me what my ambitions were, I would have said, 'to teach and to conduct a band'. I have achieved both and more. However, at the start of my career in music and education the differences between me and the majority of my peers at Bretton Hall College were vast. A gaping hole where social, cultural and educational learning should and could have been. Over the years, the holes have been filled, but those holes remain for many working class children today. What would different look like if we addressed working class questions, if we responded to old questions with new thinking?

Why are the working class not valued as partners?

If, as a nation, we cared that many children under achieve or fail we would value all parents and carers as equals in terms of the contribution they make in both the upbringing and education of their family – we would value both the knowledge parents and carers have of their children and the experiences and heritage that they can share from their communities. A simple answer to improving outcomes for all children is to engage in a partnership between parents, carers and the teaching community in a structured way. This is not an original idea but one that has failed to be embedded in a society that leaves parents and carers at the school gate, invited in for a five-minute talking to at parents evening once or twice a year, or more if their child has been excluded. Partnership – when developed and entrenched (it takes time and skill) through listening and understanding will change the view working class parents and carers have of school, increase expectations and empower them to share in the education of their child. Mutuality is central to the success of any partnership, respecting each other for the support they can provide and that will help each child to progress.

Why do working class children not achieve?

The reality is that the majority do achieve, but not necessarily at the level expected by decision makers. The need to understand how and why children can learn is fundamental to pedagogy – how teachers teach. Investment in teachers and leaders in terms of evidence based initial training and continuing professional development has been recognized since the introduction of the Masters qualification in the university sector of the 14th century[117], teaching apprenticeships in the 19th century and, more recently in Government reports. Getting it [teaching] right for the working class remains an ongoing challenge in many schools.

Given that the majority of teachers are middle class, an appropriate starting point might be to increase understanding of how working class, disadvantaged and SEND children learn, and refocusing teacher training and professional training on the majority of the population in schools, identifying what is needed to prepare children for work. It is also about changing the mindset of the adults and services around the school to improve the outcomes for all children. I have long since known that if you change the attitudes and behaviours of adults you improve the attitudes and behaviours of the child.

Why do working class families not participate fully in early years provision?

This is a common question raised by people who, through family tradition of both parents working, have the necessary resources to support their child's participation in early years education. For the working class there are two fundamental issues. One is funding and availability. Access to early years provision isn't always possible and may be limited in some areas of the country. Most working class families will access school based early years provision rather than private or independent settings.

Secondly there may be a lack of motivation underpinned by personal experience, plus a lack of understanding of what is on offer. There have been changes to two-year-old provision and an increase in hours available. This has to be understood and accessible to all families.

A third point emerges relating to the quality of provision available to have families who have some difficulties. Traditionally working class families will support each other through the extended family rather than be subject to judgements in other settings.

Sure Start Children's Centres were the main vehicles for ensuring good quality family services and provision were located in accessible places and welcoming to all. The aim for every Sure Start Centre was to improve outcomes for children and families.[118] There are some fine nursery settings that take that approach today. If we want working class families to fully participate in early years we need to see more of the same – to share the benefits of early years education by building a respectful relationship with families, and sustain that to help ensure growth and school readiness.

Why is there not the will to stop the growth of disadvantage among the working class?

Part of the problem is the context of UK poverty has changed. Poverty is no longer just an issue for people out of work or living in social housing. It impacts on people with disabilities, people who've become ill and had to give up work, people in work, young people (including some just out of university), people renting from private landlords. The drive for welfare reform has been seen as an answer to the problems of disadvantage, but it's failed to understand this changing context and so the better ways forward; better housing, investment in communities – or reinvestment where cuts have decimated good work – and a continued drive to grow employment and provide good jobs that provide an income on or above a living wage.

There is also the question of relevance. Some 70 years after the introduction of the welfare state the working class have been expected to adopt the lifestyle of the middle classes: home ownership, educational aspirations and self-sufficiency. Such changes are predicated on an understanding of what different looks like. The working class need opportunities that are relevant to their circumstances, not those that are created to make everyone the same. There is a confusion that social mobility is about class migration, rather than life improvement and an improvement of life chances.

Why is school considered not relevant by the working class?

A curriculum that is not socially and culturally relevant, that presents more barriers than opportunities will not engage children in learning. The national curriculum in England has been developed on knowledge and learning experienced by the middle class. There are solutions to this dilemma that, if implemented, would address the needs of all children. The first is to break down the barriers to learning by providing opportunities for all children to participate in social and cultural activities, sport, the arts, debating, volunteering, wider community based provision, museums, trips and much more. The second requires us to relate the curriculum to the social context of the child and their future. All communities have a rich heritage, which can provide significant resources. In terms of their future, learning about the workplace can begin in primary school, increasing ambitions, breaking down barriers, and providing relevance to learning. Increasing access to learning for all children should be the benchmark of a successful school.

Why is working class success only measured by exam results?

The annual media frenzy that follows primary phase national curriculum assessments (SATs) and secondary phase GCSE exam results only serves to remind the majority of the working class families that their children are disadvantaged, with private and grammar schools forming the majority at the top of published league tables. For the minority of working class students who do achieve, this is a demonstration that passing exams is a possibility at primary and secondary. Though recent primary SATs serve to prove the difficulties for those without the related social and cultural capital to respond to questions in the English paper. EPI Closing the Gap research[119] reminds us that it will take decades to 'close the gap'. A more meaningful assessment at secondary phase would be destination outcomes. Measuring student's outcomes by where the examinations take them. If exam results are to be a single judgment of success, all forms of examinations should be considered providing a more rounded picture of what each school has to offer.

Why is university not the answer for the majority of working class children?

This is not entirely true of all working class families; for some school has provided the social mobility referred to by politicians; access to university, improved housing and health and, ultimately, better life chances. 'Education as a 'social distributor' of life chances often compounds rather than eases the difficulties of disadvantaged children'.[120] However, it seems clear to me that for the working class majority university is not an option at the point of leaving school. There are more relevant options that would address the university question by providing all young people with the choice of further study, community service or an apprenticeship as they move into work and progress in their life. Two changes to accessing apprenticeships would increase opportunities and enhance life chances for many, by removing the requirement of a standard pass in English and maths, replacing this with Btec qualifications that demonstrate use of English and maths, and an increase in apprenticeships at aged 16. This might also address the 50 per cent or more who fail to achieve a good pass, repeating English and maths until 18 – a situation which delays rather than solves the problem of 'what next?', and may contribute to NEETs.[121,122]

Why is there a lack of ambition for the working class?

There is no evidence that the working class cannot achieve – in education, employment, housing and health. There is also no evidence that the working class are any less likely to have a desire for success than others. What we have, though, is a lack of societal ambition outside those spurious targets (like university entry) that only concern 50 per cent of the population at best. To increase ambition for the working class there needs to be a mutual understanding of what is available in terms of alternatives, and engagement with the working class about what they actually want. By talking and listening ambitions can be shared – a do *with* rather than do to approach.

We live in an increasingly complex and chaotic world that accepts failure and condones exclusion, creating a gap that exists across society. I am pushing back against any practice that does not improve the life chances of *all children* through education, parent and carer engagement and advocating for a change in routes to employability.

The Social Mobility Commission[123] emphasises the need for a more focused approach. The commission calls for the Government to invest in a ten-year plan with targets that are monitored, including considerable investment in early years rather than spending on wealthy older people; the development of the whole child rather than exam results in schools; an increase in the number of apprenticeships for young people rather than adult workers, and engagement and improvement of parenting rather than a reliance on moving from welfare to work.

Social mobility is about changing the way people think, act and engage. To understand that there is an alternative way to live, that everyone can succeed. We need to act fast and we need to act now to galvanise society to act against what is ultimately the social injustice of our time. Social Mobility Commission recommendations begin with the early years, each go part way to achieving social mobility. There is considerable evidence that an alternative way could do much more than simply continue with common practices that have had limited impact on future social mobility.

There is no evidence that the attainment gap cannot be closed for all children, regardless of background, challenge or need. To recommend a national ambition set at 50% will allow excuses and caveats; creating a barrier to change. Evidence has shown (Impetus Foundation, 2014[124], Rowntree Foundation, 2016[125], PwC, 2016[126]) that the key to change is to develop an approach that engenders self-belief, building the core in every child at the earliest stages of their development: Aspiration, 'I can', Access, 'I do', Attainment, 'I have', and Achievement, 'I am'. My recommendation is to focus childcare policy on improving teaching for the poorest children by doubling the Early Years Pupil Premium to enable childcare providers to offer extra evidence based support for disadvantaged children.

So, are the working class born to fail?

Research would indicate that rather than reducing the chances of failure within the working class over the last forty years, we have increased the possibility in housing, education and social care. This should not have happened, nor should it be allowed to continue. Back in 1973 authors of the *Born to Fail?* report referenced Tawney, 'The continuance of social evils is not due to the fact that we do not know what is right, but that we prefer to continue doing what is wrong. Those who have the power to remove them do not have the will, and those who have the will have not, as yet, the power'. The power rests within us all. With new thinking, mutuality, respect and collaboration working class children can succeed from birth, at school in post 16 study and in the workplace.

Ultimately, it is about taking responsibility, owning a shared moral purpose and shared ambition and integrity that can provide the opportunities and resources needed for all children and their families to achieve. This is social justice in action, and possibly, social mobility that really works.

The authors of the *Born to Fail?* report would never have envisaged that, more than 40 years on, we'd be having the same debate and asking the same old questions that originated in Victorian and Edwardian England. If we are to discover a lasting solution, and ensure social justice as a result, we need to come up with some new thinking and not repeat familiar actions of the past. And we need to recognise, everyone who lives in this country needs to recognise, that we all have a part to play to ensure every child across the country should have a choice, an opportunity, and a secure future. And if they're given it, every single one of us will benefit.

References

Chapter 1

1. Wedge, P. and Prosser H. (1973) *Born to Fail?* London: Arrow Books in association with The National Children's Bureau.

2. Tawney, R. H. (1912) in Rose, M. E. (1972) *The Relief of Poverty*, London: Duckworth in association with Child Poverty Action Group.

3. Social Mobility Commission (2017) 'Time for Change: An Assessment of Government Policies on Social Mobility 1997–2017', London: Social Mobility Commission. Available at: www.gov.uk/government/publications/social-mobility-policies-between-1997-and-2017-time-for-change

4. Andrews, J., Robinson, D., Hutchinson, J. (2017) 'Closing the Gap? Trends in Educational Attainment and Disadvantage', London: Education Policy Institute. Available at: https://epi.org.uk/report/closing-the-gap/

5. Department for Education (2017) 'School Workforce in England: November 2016. SFR 25/2017, 22 June 2017', Sheffield: Department for Education/Office for National Statistics. Available at: www.gov.uk/government/statistics/school-workforce-in-england-november-2016

6. Hazell, W. (2017), 'Warning of 'major' teacher recruitment crisis as trainee numbers fall by 10 per cent'. *TES*, 31 August. Available at: www.tes.com/news/school-news/breaking-news/warning-major-teacher-recruitment-crisis-trainee-numbers-fall-10-cent

7. Howson, J. (2017) 'Not a good year for ITT', 31 August 2017 Available at: https://johnohowson.wordpress.com/2017/08/31/not-a-good-year-for-itt/.

8. Social Mobility Commission (2017) 'Time for Change: An Assessment of Government Policies on Social Mobility 1997–2017', London: Social Mobility Commission. Available at: www.gov.uk/government/publications/social-mobility-policies-between-1997-and-2017-time-for-change

9. Laws, D. (2016) 'How good is a British education?' *Prospect Magazine*, 13 December 2016. Available at: www.prospectmagazine.co.uk/politics/how-good-is-a-british-education-pisa-results-maths-science

Chapter 2

10. www.gov.uk/government/speeches/justine-greening-we-should-not-accept-britain-as-it-has-been

11. The National Health Service Act 1946 (c 81) Available at: www.legislation.gov.uk/ukpga/1946/81/pdfs/ukpga_19460081_en.pdf

12. Education (No. 2) Act 1986 (c 61) Available at: www.legislation.gov.uk/ukpga/1986/61

13. Children Act 1972 (c 44) Available at: www.legislation.gov.uk/ukpga/1972/44/enacted

14. The Education and Skills Act 2008 (c 25) Available at: www.legislation.gov.uk/ukpga/2008/25/contents

15. Department for Education (2010) 'The school funding settlement for 2011-12: The pupil premium and Dedicated Schools Grant', London: Department for Education. Available at: http://media.education.gov.uk/assets/files/pdf/t/the%20school%20funding%20settlement%20for%202011%2012%20the%20pupil%20premium%20and%20dedicated%20schools%20grant.pdf

16. Children and Families Act 2014 (c 6) Available at: www.legislation.gov.uk/ukpga/2014/6/contents/enacted

17. Department of Education (2014) 'Special educational needs and disability code of practice: 0 to 25 years', London: Department for Education. Available at: www.gov.uk/government/publications/send-code-of-practice-0-to-25

18. Warnock, M. (1978) 'Special Educational Needs Report of the Committee of Enquiry into the education of handicapped children and young people'. Cmnd. 7212 London: HMSO. Available at: http://webarchive.nationalarchives.gov.uk/20101007182820/http://sen.ttrb.ac.uk/attachments/21739b8e-5245-4709-b433-c14b08365634.pdf

19. Dougherty, K. J., and Callender, C. (2017) 'English and American higher education access and completion policy regimes: similarities, differences and possible lessons Centre for Global Higher Education working paper series Working paper no. 24 August 2017', London: Centre for Global Higher Education, UCL Institute of Education Available at: www.researchcghe.org/publications/english-and-american-higher-education-access-and-completion-policy-regimes-similarities-differences-and-possible-lessons/

20. Wolf, A. (2011) 'Review of vocational education: the Wolf report', London: Department for Business, Innovation & Skills and Department for Education Available at: www.gov.uk/government/publications/review-of-vocational-education-the-wolf-report

21. UCL (2013) The Erikson-Goldthorpe Scheme. Available at: www.ucl.ac.uk/celsius/online-training/socio/se050200

22. BBC (2013), Great British Class Survey: www.bbc.co.uk/labuk/experiments/the-great-british-class-survey

23. Goldthorpe, J. (2016) 'Social class mobility in modern Britain: changing structure, constant process'. [Lecture to The British Academy]. London 15 March 2016. Text Available at: www.britac.ac.uk/sites/default/files/05%20Goldthorpe%201825.pdf

Chapter 3

24. Mulcahy, E., Baars, S., Bowen-Viner, K., Menzies, L. (2017) 'The underrepresentation of Gypsy, Roma and Traveller pupils in higher education. A report on barriers from early years to secondary and beyond',London: King's College London. Available at: https://cdn.lkmco.org/wp-content/uploads/2017/07/KINGWIDE_28494_brief_proof2.pdf

25. Department for Education (2012) 'Government publishes destination data for the first time', DfE 17 July 2012. Available at: www.gov.uk/government/news/government-publishes-destination-data-for-the-first-time

26. Office for Fair Access (2017) 'Outcomes of access agreement monitoring for 2015-16', Bristol: OFFA. Available at: www.offa.org.uk/wp-content/uploads/2017/06/OFFA-Monitoring-Outcomes-Report-2015-16-Final.pdf

27. Turner, C. (2017) 'Number of poor students dropping out of university at highest level in five years', *The Telegraph*, 29 June 2017. Available at: www.telegraph.co.uk/news/2017/06/28/number-poor-students-dropping-university-highest-level-five/

28. Teach First (2017) 'Beyond Access: Getting to University and Succeeding There', London: Teach First/Credit Suisse EMEA Foundation. Available at: www.teachfirst.org.uk/sites/default/files/TF--CTI%20UNI%20Report%20 DIGITAL.pdf

29. Sundorph, E., Vasilev, D. and Coiffait, L. (2017) 'Joining the elite: how top universities can enhance social mobility', London: Reform. Available at: www.reform.uk/wp-content/uploads/2017/09/Joining-The-Elite-how-top-universities-can-enhance-social-mobility.pdf

30. Barton, G. (2017) 'Results day: 'As our country becomes more insular, so, it seems, does its curriculum'.', *TES*, 17 August 2017. Available at: www.tes.com/news/school-news/breaking-views/results-day-our-country-becomes-more-insular-so-it-seems-does-its

31. BBC The Listening Project (2017), Available at: www.bbc.co.uk/programmes/b091sw4d

32. www.gov.uk/government/publications/higher-and-degree-apprenticeships

33. Chartered Management Institute (2017) 'Slow Growth In Parents' Awareness Of Degree Apprenticeships Means Their Children May Be Missing Out', Available at: www.managers.org.uk/insights/research/current-research/2017/august/the-age-of-apprenticeships?utm_campaign=Age_of_Apprenticeships_2017&utm_source=FE_News&utm_medium=referral

34. Williams, J. C. (2017) *White Working Class – Overcoming Class Cluelessness in America*, Boston: Harvard Business Press.

35. Vance, J. D. (2016) *Hillbilly Elegy, A Memoir of a Family and Culture in Crisis*, London: William Collins.

36. Teach First (2017) 'Beyond Access: Getting to University and Succeeding There', London: Teach First/Credit Suisse EMEA Foundation. Available at: www.teachfirst.org.uk/sites/default/files/TF--CTI%20UNI%20Report%20 DIGITAL.pdf

37. Social Mobility Commission (2017) 'Time for Change: An Assessment of Government Policies on Social Mobility 1997–2017', London: Social Mobility Commission. Available at: www.gov.uk/government/publications/social-mobility-policies-between-1997-and-2017-time-for-change

38. Mckenzie, L (2016) 'Brexit is the only way the working class can change anything', *The Guardian*, 15 June 2016. Available at: www.theguardian.com/commentisfree/2016/jun/15/brexit-working-class-sick-racist-eu-referendum

39. Freedland, J. (2017) 'Grenfell Tower will forever stand as a rebuke to the right', *The Guardian*, 16 June 2017. Available at: www.theguardian.com/commentisfree/2017/jun/16/grenfell-tower-rebuke-right-rampant-inequality

40. Blunkett, D. (2015) 'Labour's Sure Start scheme was a huge success – we can learn from this in London,' *The Independent*, 7 August 2015. Available at: www.independent.co.uk/voices/comment/labours-sure-start-scheme-was-a-huge-success-we-can-learn-from-this-in-london-10445314.html

41. Ofsted (2013) 'The pupil premium: how schools are spending the funding successfully', Manchester: Ofsted. Available at: www.gov.uk/government/publications/the-pupil-premium-how-schools-are-spending-the-funding-successfully

42. Department for Education and Department of Health (2014) 'SEND code of practice: 0 to 25 years', London: Department for Education and Department of Health. Available at: www.gov.uk/government/publications/send-code-of-practice-0-to-25

43. Achievement for All (2016) 'Our Impact', Available at: https://afaeducation.org/our-impact/

44. Sharples, J., Slavin, R., Chambers, B. and Sharp, C. (2011) 'Effective Classroom Strategies for Closing the Gap in Educational Achievement for Children and Young People Living in Poverty, Including White Working Class Boys', London: Centre for Excellence and Outcomes in Children and Young People's Services. Available at: www.york.ac.uk/media/iee/documents/Closing%20the%20Gap.pdf

45. Ofsted (2013) 'The pupil premium: how schools are spending the funding successfully', Manchester: Ofsted. Available at: www.gov.uk/government/publications/the-pupil-premium-how-schools-are-spending-the-funding-successfully

Chapter 4

46. Donnelly, L. (2016) 'Smoking ban sees 40 per cent cut in heart attacks in UK since 2007 law was introduced', *The Telegraph*. 4 Feb 2016 Available at: www.telegraph.co.uk/news/health/news/12138413/Smoking-ban-sees-40-per-cent-cut-in-heart-attacks-since-2007-law-was-introduced.html

47. Department for Transport (2001) Think! Campaign. Available at: http://think.direct.gov.uk/seat-belts.html

48. Lullaby Trust (2017) 'Rates of SIDS reach new record low but The Lullaby Trust warns against complacency', Available at: www.lullabytrust.org.uk/ons-2015/

49, Impetus (2014) 'Make Neets History in 2014', London: Impetus. Available at: http://impetus-pef.org.uk/wp-content/uploads/2013/12/Make-NEETs-History-Report_ImpetusPEF_January-2014.pdf

50. Public Health England (2016) 'Public Health and NHS Outcomes Frameworks for Children', Available at: http://fingertips.phe.org.uk/cyphof

Chapter 5

51. 'Britain, the great meritocracy: Prime Minister's speech', 9 September, 2016. Available at: www.gov.uk/government/speeches/britain-the-great-meritocracy-prime-ministers-speech

52. Kirby, P. and Cullinane, C. (2016) 'Class differences: Ethnicity and disadvantage', London: The Sutton Trust. Available at: www.suttontrust.com/research-paper/class-differences-ethnicity-and-disadvantage/

53. Raising the Achievement of all Learners in Inclusive Education Website Available at: www.european-agency.org/agency-projects/raising-achievement

54. Andrews, J., Robinson, D., Hutchinson, J. (2017) 'Closing the Gap? Trends in Educational Attainment and Disadvantage', London: Education Policy Institute. Available at: https://epi.org.uk/report/closing-the-gap/

55. Save the Children (2016) 'Untapped Potential: How England's nursery lottery is failing too many children', London: Save the Children. Available at: www.savethechildren.org.uk/sites/default/files/docs/Untapped_Potential.pdf

56. Knowles, C. (2017) 'Closing the attainment gap in maths: a study of good practice in early years and primary settings', London: Fair Education Alliance. Available at: https://static1.squarespace.com/static/543e665de4b0fbb2b140b291/t/58aaeac429687f223f0ff369/1487596235907/FEA+Numeracy+Report_FV.pdf

57. Neston High Wirral case study featured in Blandford, S. (2015) *Love to Teach*, Woodbridge: John Catt Educational

58. Desforges C. with Abouchaar, A., (2003) 'The Impact of Parental Involvement, Parental Support and Family Education on Pupil Achievement and Adjustment: A Literature Review', DfES Research Report 433, 2003. Available at: http://webarchive.nationalarchives.gov.uk/20130403234550/https://www.education.gov.uk/publications/eOrderingDownload/RR433.pdf

59. Social Mobility Commission (2017) 'Time for Change: An Assessment of Government Policies on Social Mobility 1997–2017', London: Social Mobility Commission. Available at: www.gov.uk/government/publications/social-mobility-policies-between-1997-and-2017-time-for-change

60 Lyng Hall Secondary School Case Study featured in Blandford, S. (2015) *Take the Lead*, Woodbridge: John Catt Educational

61. Achievement for All (2017) 'Achieving Early'. Available at: https:// afaeducation.org/our-programmes/early-years-achieving-early-and-firm-foundation/working-together/

62. Lamb, B. (2009) 'Lamb Inquiry Special Educational Needs and Parental Confidence. Annesley', DCSF Publications. Available at: http://webarchive. nationalarchives.gov.uk/20130320215632/https://www.education.gov.uk/ publications/standard/publicationDetail/Page1/DCSF-01143-2009

63. Social Mobility Commission (2017) 'Time for Change: An Assessment of Government Policies on Social Mobility 1997–2017', London: Social Mobility Commission. Available at: www.gov.uk/government/publications/social-mobility-policies-between-1997-and-2017-time-for-change

64. Blandford, S (2017), 'Promoting social mobility early', *Children and Young People Now*, 26 July 2017. Available at: www.cypnow.co.uk/cyp/analysis/2003965/ promoting-social-mobility-early

65 European Agency for Special Needs and Inclusive Education (2016) 'Raising the Achievement of All Learners in Inclusive Education – Literature Review', Odense/Brussels: European Agency for Special Needs and Inclusive Education. Available at: www.european-agency.org/sites/default/files/Raising%20 Achievement%20%C2%AD%20Literature%20Review.pdf

66. Carers Trust Website: https://carers.org/

67. Sempik, J. and Becker, S (2013) 'Young Adult Carers at School: Experiences and Perceptions of Caring and Education', London: Carers Trust / Nottingham University. Available at: https://carers.org/sites/files/carerstrust/young_adult_ carers_at_school-8_11_13-1_proof_4_final_1.pdf

68. Sharples, J., Webster, R. and Blatchford, P. (2015) 'Making Best Use of Teaching Assistants Guidance Report', London: Education Endowment Foundation. Available at: https://v1.educationendowmentfoundation.org.uk/ uploads/pdf/Making_best_use_of_TAs_printable.pdf

69. Youth Sports Trust Team Leader Programme Website: https://www. youthsporttrust.org/team-leaders

Chapter 6

(70) Education Endowment Foundation (2017) 'Achieve Together', London: Education Endowment Foundation. Available at: https://educationendowmentfoundation.org.uk/our-work/projects/achieve-together

71. Sellen, P. (2016) 'Teacher workload and professional development in England's secondary schools insights from TALIS', London: Education Policy Institute. Available at: https://epi.org.uk/report/teacherworkload/

72. National Union of Teachers (2016) 'NUT Young Teachers Working Party survey', Available at: www.teachers.org.uk/sites/default/files2014/nut-young-teachers-survey-questions-final.doc See also: www.teachers.org.uk/news-events/conference-2017/workload-driving-young-teachers-out-profession

73. Menzies, L., *et al* (2015) 'Why Teach?', LKMco. Available at: http://whyteach.lkmco.org/wp-content/uploads/2015/10/Embargoed-until-Friday-23-October-2015-Why-Teach.pdf

74. Cordingley *et al* (2015) 'Developing Great Teaching: Lessons from the international reviews into effective professional development', London: Teacher Development Trust. Available at: http://tdtrust.org/about/dgt

75. Department for Education (2017) 'School Workforce in England: November 2016', SFR 25/2017, 22 June 2017. Sheffield: Department for Education/Office for National Statistics. Available at: www.gov.uk/government/statistics/school-workforce-in-england-november-2016

76. Education Endowment Foundation (2016) 'RETAIN: Early Career Teachers CPD'. Available at: https://educationendowmentfoundation.org.uk/our-work/projects/cornwall-college-retain

77. Bedell, G (2016) 'Teenage Mental Health Crisis', *The Independent*, 27 February 2016. Available at: www.independent.co.uk/life-style/health-and-families/features/teenage-mental-health-crisis-rates-of-depression-have-soared-in-the-past-25-years-a6894676.html

78. Self-Harm UK/Youthscape (2017) 'The facts: Self-harm statistics'. Available at: https://www.selfharm.co.uk/get/facts/self-harm_statistics

79. Carrington, H (2014) 'More than half of bullied children become depressed as adults, survey shows', *The Independent*, 10 June 2014 Available at: www.independent.co.uk/life-style/health-and-families/health-news/more-than-half-of-bullied-children-become-depressed-as-adults-survey-shows-9523967.html

80. Place2be Wesbite: https://www.place2be.org.uk/

81. Ofsted (2013) 'The pupil premium: how schools are spending the funding successfully', Manchester: Ofsted. Available at: www.gov.uk/government/publications/the-pupil-premium-how-schools-are-spending-the-funding-successfully

82. Gorard, S. (2017) 'Exploring Recruitment, Retention and Region', BERA Conference Presentation. 12 June 2017. Plymouth University.

83. Public Health England (2016) 'Public Health and NHS Outcomes Frameworks for Children'. Available at: http://fingertips.phe.org.uk/cyphof

84. Layard, R. *et al* (2014) 'What predicts a successful life? A life-course model of well-being.' *The Economic Journal,* 124 (580). F720-F738. ISSN 1468-0297

85. O'Brien, J. (2016) 'Anthony got two Fs in his GCSEs: that may not seem earth-shattering to you, but to him – and to me – that represents a triumph', *Times Educational Supplement,* 25 August 2016. Available at: www.tes.com/news/school-news/breaking-views/anthony-got-two-fs-his-gcses-may-not-seem-earth-shattering-you-him

86. National Literacy Trust: Read On. Get On Campaign. Available at: https://literacytrust.org.uk/policy-and-campaigns/read-on-get-on/

87. Education Reform Act 1988 (c 40) Available at: www.legislation.gov.uk/ukpga/1988/40/contents

88. Maslow, A. (1943) 'A Theory of Human Motivation', *Psychological Review,* 50(4), pp.370-396.

89 Ford, T., Parker, C., Salim, J., Goodman, R., Logan, S. & Henley, W. (2017) 'The relationship between exclusion from school and mental health: A secondary analysis of the British Child and Adolescent Mental Health Surveys 2004 and 2007', *Psychological Medicine,* 1-13. doi:10.1017/S003329171700215X

90. Department for Education (2017) 'Permanent and fixed-period exclusions in England: 2015 to 2016', Sheffield: Department for Education/Office for National Statistics. Available at: www.gov.uk/government/statistics/school-workforce-in-england-november-2016

91. IPPR (2017) 'Half of expelled pupils suffer mental health issues in 'burningly injust system', think-tank finds', 20 July 2017. Available at: www.ippr.org/news-and-media/press-releases/half-of-expelled-pupils-suffer-mental-health-issues-in-burningly-injust-system-think-tank-finds

92. The Fair Education Alliance (2017) 'Report Card 2016/17', London: The Fair Education Alliance. Available at: www.faireducation.org.uk/report-card/

93. Staufenberg, J. (2017) 'Half of permanently excluded pupils have a mental illness, report finds', *Schools Week,* July 20 2017 Available at: http://schoolsweek. co.uk/half-of-permanently-excluded-pupils-have-a-mental-illness-report-finds

94. Evans, J. (2010) 'Not present and not correct: Understanding and preventing school exclusions', Ilford: Barnardos. Available at: www.barnardos.org.uk/ not_present_and_not_correct.pdf

95. Knuutila, A. (2010) 'Punishing Costs: How Locking Up Children Is Making Britain Less Safe', London: New Economics Foundation. Available at: http:// neweconomics.org/2010/03/punishing-costs/

Chapter 7

96. Waldfogel, J. and Washbrook, E (2010) 'Low income and early cognitive development in the U.K. A Report for the Sutton Trust', London: Sutton Trust. Available at: www.suttontrust.com/wp-content/uploads/2010/02/Sutton_ Trust_Cognitive_Report.pdf

97. The All-Party Parliamentary Group On Social Mobility (2012) '7 Truths About Social Mobility'. Available at: www.raeng.org.uk/publications/other/7-key-truths-about-social-mobility

98. Fair Education Alliance Report Cards are available at: www.faireducation. org.uk/report-card/

99. Department for Education (2015) 'Nutbrown review – Foundations for Quality', London: Department for Education. Available at: www.gov.uk/ government/publications/nutbrown-review-foundations-for-quality

100. Save the Children (2016) 'Untapped potential: how England's nursery lottery is failing too many children', London: Save the Children. Available at: www.savethechildren.org.uk/sites/default/files/images/Untapped_Potential. pdf

101. Achievement for All (2017) 'Achieving Early.' Available at: https:// afaeducation.org/our-programmes/early-years-achieving-early-and-firm-foundation/working-together/

102. Nursery World (2015) 'Winners of the Nursery World Awards 2015'. Available at: www.nurseryworld.co.uk/nursery-world/news/1153904/winners-of-the-nursery-world-awards-2015

103. Warnock, M. (1978) 'Special Educational Needs Report of the Committee of Enquiry into the education of handicapped children and young people', Cmnd. 7212 London: HMSO. Available at: http://webarchive.nationalarchives. gov.uk/20101007182820/http://sen.ttrb.ac.uk/attachments/21739b8e-5245-4709-b433-c14b08365634.pdf

104. UNESCO (1994) 'The Salamanca Statement on Principles, Policy and Practice in Special Needs Education', Paris, France: UNESCO. Available at: www.unesco.org/education/pdf/SALAMA_E.PDF

105. UNESCO (2005) 'Guidelines for Inclusion: Ensuring Access to Education for All', Paris, France: UNESCO. Available at: http://unesdoc.unesco.org/images/0014/001402/140224e.pdf

106. Centre for Studies on Inclusive Education (2015) 'What is Inclusion?' Available at: www.csie.org.uk/inclusion/what.shtml

107. Department for Education (2017) 'Special educational needs in England: January 2017', Sheffield: Department for Education / Office for National Statistics. Available at: www.gov.uk/government/uploads/system/uploads/attachment_data/file/633031/SFR37_2017_Main_Text.pdf

108. Ofsted (2010) 'The special educational needs and disability review', Manchester: Ofsted. Available at: www.gov.uk/government/publications/special-educational-needs-and-disability-review

109. National College for Teaching and Leadership (2014) 'National Award for Special Educational Needs Co-ordinator: learning outcomes. NCTL'. Available at: www.gov.uk/government/publications/national-award-for-sen-co-ordination-learning-outcomes

110. Lereya, S., *et al.* (2015) 'Adult mental health consequences of peer bullying and maltreatment in childhood: two cohorts in two countries', *The Lancet Psychiatry*, Volume 2 , Issue 6 , 524–531. Available at: www.thelancet.com/journals/lanpsy/article/PIIS2215-0366(15)00165-0/fulltext

111. Office for National Statistics (2017) 'UK labour market: August 2017', Newport: Office for National Statistics. Available at: www.ons.gov.uk/employmentandlabourmarket/peopleinwork/employmentandemployeetypes/bulletins/uklabourmarket/august2017

112. D'Arcy, C. and Hurrell, A. (2014) 'Escape Plan: Understanding Who Progresses from Low Pay and Who Gets Stuck', London: Resolution Foundation. Available at: www.resolutionfoundation.org/app/uploads/2014/11/Escape-Plan.pdf

113. Department for Business, Energy & Industrial Strategy (2017)'Good work: the Taylor review of modern working practices', London: Department for Business, Energy & Industrial Strategy. Available at: www.gov.uk/government/publications/good-work-the-taylor-review-of-modern-working-practices

114. CBI/Pearson (2017) 'Education and Skills Survey: Helping the UK Thrive', London: Pearson. Available at: http://go.international.ac.uk/cbipearson-education-and-skills-survey-2017-helping-uk-thrive

115. The Social Mobility Commission (2017) 'Social Mobility Employer Index'. Available at: www.socialmobility.org.uk/wp-content/uploads/2017/06/Top-50-.pdf

116. Department for Education (2017) 'Education Secretary announces 6 new opportunity areas', DfE, 18 January 2017 Available at: www.gov.uk/government/news/education-secretary-announces-6-new-opportunity-areas

Chapter 8

117. De Ridder-Symoens, H. (ed) (1991), *A History of the University in Europe: Volume 1, Universities in the Middle Ages,* Cambridge: Cambridge University Press.

118. House of Commons Library (2017) 'Sure Start (England) Briefing Paper Number 7257', 9 June 2017. Available at: http://researchbriefings.parliament.uk/ResearchBriefing/Summary/CBP-7257#fullreport

119. Andrews, J., Robinson, D., Hutchinson, J. (2017) 'Closing the Gap? Trends in Educational Attainment and Disadvantage', London: Education Policy Institute. Available at: https://epi.org.uk/report/closing-the-gap/

120. Wedge, P. and Prosser, H. (1973), *Born to Fail?*: The National Children's Bureau reports on striking differences in the lives of British. London: Arrow Books.

121. Adams, R., Weale, S., Bengtsson, H. (2017), 'Proportion of students getting good GCSE grades falls after reforms', *The Guardian*, 24 August 2017. Available at: www.theguardian.com/education/2017/aug/24/proportion-of-students-getting-good-gcse-grades-falls-after-reforms

122. Department for Education (2017) 'Statistics: NEET and participation', Sheffield: Department for Education. Available at: www.gov.uk/government/collections/statistics-neet

123. Social Mobility Commission (2017) 'Time for Change: An Assessment of Government Policies on Social Mobility 1997–2017', London: Social Mobility Commission. Available at: www.gov.uk/government/publications/social-mobility-policies-between-1997-and-2017-time-for-change

124. Impetus (2014) 'Make Neets History in 2014', London: Impetus Available at: http://impetus-pef.org.uk/wp-content/uploads/2013/12/Make-NEETs-History-Report_ImpetusPEF_January-2014.pdf

125. Tinson, A. *et al.* (2016) 'Monitoring poverty and social exclusion 2016', York: Joseph Rowntree Foundation. Available at: www.jrf.org.uk/report/monitoring-poverty-and-social-exclusion-2016

126. PwC (2016) 'Achieving Schools: Social Impact Assessment Final Report 2016', London: PwC. Available at: https://www.paperturn-view.com/flipbook/id/achievement-for-all/achieving-schools-social-impact-assessment-pwc?pid=NzY7665

Acknowledgements

Jenny Hulme has contributed so much in ordering my thoughts, which have been evolving for over five decades. I am indebted to her as a writing partner and friend, who knows how to communicate the issues introduced in this book, making sense of the challenges and ideas.

In contrast to the longevity of my experiences, this book has been written in a relatively short space of time. Much of the content has been shared with others, each of their corrections and comments has been invaluable. Stefan Burkey, born into a working class family, experiencing homelessness during a critical period of his life – your comments and contribution to the text have been affirming.

My Achievement for All colleagues – Marius Frank (former headteacher and CEO of ASDAN; award winning programme leader), Dr Catherine Knowles (author, teacher and community leader), Mark Jamieson (business leader and coach), Laura Bromberg (former headteacher; national advisor and business leader) and Maureen Hunt (former headteacher; local authority advisor; award-winning programme leader; and author – each taking time out of their summer holidays to review and contribute to the text; questioning my assertions enabling class consciousness to sing. This entailed late nights and early mornings, sharing their commitment and moral purpose to improve outcomes for all children.

Laura Smith, from Consillium Communications, advising on the clarity of the text. As a former BBC communications professional, Laura's analysis has been incredibly helpful.

The Right Honorable David Laws (former Minister for Schools and now, Executive Chairman, Education Policy Institute), for his valued support.

Alex Sharratt, at John Catt, for your unfailing support in publishing this book, without any question or hesitation. I hope that your team will welcome this work to their catalogue.

Susan Blandford, my twin, who shared many of my early experiences mentioned has commented freely on the content, addressing minor memory lapses, whilst proclaiming that there is more (much more) to be said if we are to understand how the working class can achieve.

As always, I am indebted to my family, Charlie, Bethany and Mia for the love and support they give.

Further reading

Blandford, S. (2017) *Achievement for All in International Classrooms*, London: Bloomsbury Publishing.

Blandford, S. and Knowles, C. (2016) *Developing Professional Practice 0-7*, (2nd Edition), Abingdon: Routledge.

Blandford, S. (2015) *Don't Like Mondays?* Woodbridge: John Catt.

Blandford, S. (2015) *Make School Better*, Woodbridge: John Catt.

Blandford, S. (2015) *Love to Teach: Bring out the best in you and your class*, Woodbridge: John Catt.

Blandford, S. (2015), *Take the Lead*, Woodbridge: John Catt.

Blandford, S. and Knowles, C. (2013) *Achievement for All: Raising Aspirations, Access and Achievement*, London: Bloomsbury.